Hyperculture

Byung-Chul Han

Hyperculture
Culture and Globalization

Translated by Daniel Steuer

polity

Originally published in German as *Hyperkulturalität: Kultur und Globalisierung*
© Merve Verlag, 2005

This English edition © Polity Press, 2022

Excerpt from: Peter Handke, *Am Felsfenster morgens (und andere Ortszeiten 1982–1987)*
© Suhrkamp Verlag, Berlin, 2019

Excerpt from: Peter Handke, *Phantasien der Wiederholung* © Suhrkamp Verlag,
Frankfurt am Main, 1983. All rights reserved by and controlled through Suhrkamp
Verlag.

Polity Press
65 Bridge Street
Cambridge CB2 1UR, UK

Polity Press
101 Station Landing
Suite 300
Medford, MA 02155, USA

ISBN-13: 978-1-5095-4616-9
ISBN-13: 978-1-5095-4617-6 (paperback)

A catalogue record for this book is available from the British Library.

Library of Congress Control Number: 2021942107

Typeset in 11.5 on 15 pt Janson Text
by Cheshire Typesetting Ltd, Cuddington, Cheshire
Printed and bound in Great Britain by TJ Books Ltd, Padstow, Cornwall

Excerpt from: Peter Handke, Phantasien der Wiederholung. © Suhrkamp Verlag
Frankfurt am Main
1983. Alle Rechte bei und vorbehalten durch Suhrkamp Verlag Berlin.
Excerpt from: Peter Handke, Am Felsfenster morgens (und andere Ortszeiten 1982–
1987). ©
Suhrkamp Verlag Berlin 2019.

The publisher has used its best endeavours to ensure that the URLs for external
websites referred to in this book are correct and active at the time of going to press.
However, the publisher has no responsibility for the websites and can make no
guarantee that a site will remain live or that the content is or will remain appropriate.

Every effort has been made to trace all copyright holders, but if any have been
overlooked the publisher will be pleased to include any necessary credits in any
subsequent reprint or edition.

For further information on Polity, visit our website:
politybooks.com

Contents

But the fear of the new is often as strong as the fear of the void, even when the new is the overcoming of the void. That explains why the many only see absurd chaos where a new meaning seeks to introduce its order. Indeed, the old nomos is fading away, dragging the whole system of redundant standards, norms, and traditions with it in its fall. But what is coming is not therefore devoid of standards, is not a pure nothingness, inimical to any nomos. Even in the fiercest struggle between old and new forces just standards emerge and meaningful proportions form.

Here, too, are gods that rule.
Ample are their bounds.

Carl Schmitt[1]

Tourist in a Hawaiian Shirt

Where do you want to go today?

Microsoft

The British ethnologist Nigel Barley once expressed the suspicion that 'the true key to the future' was 'that fundamental concepts such as culture will cease to exist'. We are all, Barley said, 'more or less tourists in Hawaiian shirts'.[1] After the end of culture, should the new human being simply be called 'tourist'? Or are we at long last living in a culture that affords us the freedom to spread into the wide open world? If we are, how might we describe this new culture?

Culture as Home

In his *Lectures on the Philosophy of History*, Hegel offers the following remark on the genesis of Greek culture: 'We have just spoken of heterogeneity [*Fremdartigkeit*] as an element of the Greek Spirit, and it is well known that the rudiments of Greek civilization are connected with the advent of foreigners.' It was thus the 'advent of foreigners' that constituted Greek culture. With 'grateful recollection', he says, the Greeks preserved the arrival of the foreigners in their mythology.[1] Prometheus, for instance, originates from the Caucasus. The Greek people developed 'from a *colluvies*'.[2] The original meaning of 'colluvies' is mud, filth, hotchpotch, confusion, or muddle.

According to Hegel, it is 'a superficial and absurd idea that such a beautiful and truly free life can be produced by a process so incomplex as the development of a race keeping within the limits of blood-relationship and friendship'. Rather, the 'inherent heterogeneity [*Fremdartigkeit in sich selbst*]' of spirit is that 'through which alone it acquires the power of realizing itself as Spirit'.[3] Still, heterogeneity by itself does not produce the 'beautiful free Greek spirit'. For that, what is also required is the 'overcoming' of heterogeneity. The fact that it is necessary to overcome heterogeneity, however, does not imply that it is something purely negative that might as well have been absent, for heterogeneity is in itself part of the '*elementary character* of Greek spirit'.[4] From this perspective, the presence of the foreign is necessary for the formation of one's own.

In his description of the historical development of the Greek world, Hegel obviously tries to do justice to the fact that the foreign, heterogeneity itself, has a constitutive effect. With regard to the identity of *European* culture, however, he adopts an altogether different tone. Here, he emphatically invokes the idea of Europe as 'home'. The Europeans might have taken their religion from the East, but all that satisfies their 'spiritual life' [*geistiges Leben*] they received from Greece: 'The name of Greece evokes feelings of home in the educated men in Europe, especially in us Germans.'[5] There is no longer any talk about heterogeneity in itself. The foreign is now degraded and becomes pure 'matter'. Before, heterogeneity had been a *spiritual* element, a form. But once 'European humanity came to be at home with itself', the 'historical and that which is of foreign derivation' was shaken off for good.[6] This being-at-home-with-oneself is a happy state: 'In ordinary life we like best the men and families that are homely and contented in themselves, not desiring what is outside and above them, and so it is with the Greeks.'[7]

3

Happiness is conceived as a phenomenon associated with the family, the homeland and household. It originates from a 'not outside, not beyond', from the site. In this sense, *site* is a synonym for 'spirit' [*Geist*].

Given his genealogical-historical realization that the formation of Greek culture was owed to the arrival of foreigners, or to heterogeneity in itself, Hegel's emphasis on the native home is disconcerting. It seems as though history does not coincide with that *historical moment* which produces one's own: the site in the proper sense. There is no longer any mention of the fact that 'blood-relationship' or 'friendship' leads to an impoverishment of spirit. Rather, Hegel evokes images of home, family and fatherland. What matters is being 'homely and contented' in oneself. As far as European culture is concerned, Hegel's 'spirit' has apparently rid itself of that 'heterogeneity in itself' which once provided it with 'the power of realizing itself as Spirit'. There is no longer any foreign culture, no 'arrival of foreigners' that would pull the Europeans out of their happy 'not outside, not beyond'. Thus, European culture becomes self-contented. It is satisfied with itself. There is no heterogeneity in itself to irritate it. According to Hegel's own theory, however, this would lead to a spiritual rigor mortis.

In his *Outlines of a Philosophy of the History of Man*, Herder remarks that 'all the cultivation of the east, west, and north of Europe, is a plant sprung from roman, greek, and arabic feed'.[8] In this view, European culture is anything but 'pure'. It is a bastard culture. Herder does not set out to produce a theory that has impurity as the constitutive element of culture, but at least he arrives at a concept of culture according to which any judgemental comparisons between cultures are dubious. In *Another Philosophy of History*, Herder remarks that the 'good' is 'distributed among a thousand shapes' and '*dispersed* throughout the earth'.[9] Thus, 'all comparison becomes futile'.[10] But every culture tends to take its particular perspective as absolute and is thus incapable, Herder says, of seeing what goes beyond its own position. It responds with '*contempt and disgust*' to the foreign, which is 'already *sickness*'. But it is precisely this '*blindness*' that makes it '*happy*'; that is, the formation of a happy identity requires a blindness. 'National happiness' emerges because the 'soul' forgets the '*manifold* dispositions' that dwell within it and elevates a part of itself to the status of the whole. Out of some 'awakened tones', Herder says, 'the soul soon creates a *concert*', and it no longer senses those that are not awakened, even though 'they *support* the ringing songs *silently* and in the dark'. Thus, the happiness of the 'soul' depends on a deafness.[11]

Are we today approaching a culture that is no longer characterized by the deafness and blindness on which happiness depends, a culture that, expressed in acoustic terms, has become a boundless, even site-less, hypercultural acoustic space in which the most diverse sounds are jammed together side by side? The hypercultural condition of the 'side by side', of simultaneity and of the 'as well as', would change the topology of happiness.

'National happiness', the 'song' of the 'soul' that creates happiness, is probably unknown to the tourists in Hawaiian shirts. Their happiness is of an altogether different kind; it is a happiness that emerges from an abolition of facticity, a removal of the attachment to the 'here', the site. In their case, the foreign is not 'sickness'.

5

It is something *new* to be appropriated. The tourists in Hawaiian shirts inhabit a world that unbounds itself, a hypermarket of culture, a hyperspace of possibilities. Are they less happy than the souls that make up a nation or populate a homeland? Is their form of life less desirable than that of the others? Does the abolition of facticity not lead to an increased freedom? Is the tourist in the Hawaiian shirt not the embodiment of the future happiness of *homo liber*? Or is happiness a phenomenon associated, ultimately, with boundaries and sites? And if it is, should we also expect the emergence of a new age of natives, hermits, ascetics and site fundamentalists?

Hypertext and Hyperculture

Ted Nelson, the inventor of hypertext, does not see hypertext as a phenomenon limited to digital text. The world itself is a hypertext. Hypertextuality is the 'real structure of things'.[1] 'Everything is', as Nelson's famous phrase has it, 'deeply intertwingled'.[2] Everything is tied up, networked with everything else. There are no isolated beings: 'In an important sense there are', Nelson holds, 'no subjects at all'.[3] Neither the body nor thinking follows a linear pattern: 'Unfortunately, for thousands of years the idea of sequence has been too much with us . . . *The structure of ideas* is never sequential; and indeed, our thought processes are not very sequential either.'[4] The structure of thought is an 'interwoven system of ideas (what I like to call a structangle)'.[5] A *tangle* is something jumbled up or tied into a knot. Despite its complexity, the net-like structure of reality is not chaotic. This is what the 'struct' in structangle expresses: it is a structured tangle. Linear and hierarchical structures or closed, unchanging identities are the result of compulsion: 'Hierarchical and sequential structures . . . are usually forced and artificial.'[6] Hypertext promises a liberation from compulsion. What Nelson imagines is a hypertextual universe, a network without centre, in which everything is wedded together: 'The real dream is for "everything" to be in the hypertext.'[7]

Nelson calls his hypertextual system 'Xanadu', the name of the legendary place in Asia where the powerful ruler Kubla Khan created a magnificent pleasure palace in the middle of a glorious garden. The English poet Samuel Taylor Coleridge describes this mythological place in his unfinished poem *Kubla Khan*. Nelson must have been fascinated by Coleridge's vision. In *CompLib/ Dream Machines*, he explicitly refers to Coleridge's fragment of a dream.[8] Nelson's hypertext, his 'Xanadu', thus has something dreamlike about it.

Nelson also drew sketches of his Xanadu palace. In front of the entrance to the monumental castle-like building, an oversized X stretches up to the sky. The golden X in front of every Xanadu branch bears a certain resemblance to McDonald's golden arches. The users who enter it are tellingly called 'travellers', and they are hungry: 'The Golden X's welcome the mindhungry traveller.'[9] The hungry travellers are greeted with a 'hyperwelcome' in the hypermarket of knowledge and information.

The 'intertwingularity' and the 'structangle' are also characteristic of culture today. Culture has increasingly lost the kind of structure familiar to us from conventional texts or books. There are no stories, no theology, no teleology to give it the appearance of a meaningful, homogeneous unity. The borders or enclosures that convey a semblance of cultural authenticity or genuineness are dissolving. Culture is bursting at the seams, so to speak. It is exploding all ties and joints. It is becoming unbound, un-restricted, un-ravelled: a hyperculture.[10] The hyperspace of culture is organized not by borders but by links and network connections.

The process of globalization, accelerated by the new technologies, *de-distances* cultural space. The resulting closeness creates a richness, a corpus of cultural lifeworld practices and forms of expression. The process of globalization accumulates and condenses. Heterogeneous cultural contents are pushed together side by side. Cultural spaces overlap and penetrate each other. This unbounding also applies to time. Not only different sites but also different time frames are de-*distanced* so that the different is placed side by side. The feeling of hyper-, rather than the feeling of trans-, inter- or multi-, is the most precise expression of today's culture. Cultures implode; that is, they are de-*distanced* into a hyperculture.

In a certain sense, hyperculture means *more* culture. By being de-naturalized, by being liberated from 'blood' and 'soil', that is, from biological or terrestrial codes, culture becomes genuinely cultural, even *hyper*cultural. De-naturalization intensifies culturalization. If the factual existence of a culture is tied to a site, then hyperculturalization represents an abolition of the facticity of culture.

Will hyperculture come to be seen as a fleeting semblance, a dream vision, like Coleridge's 'Xanadu'? Kubla Khan's pleasure-dome is erected on an earth that is 'with ceaseless turmoil seething'. And the sacred river 'Alph', flowing through the paradisiacal garden, sinks 'in tumult to a lifeless ocean':

> In Xanadu did Kubla Khan
> A stately pleasure-dome decree:
> Where Alph, the sacred river, ran
> Through caverns measureless to man
>   Down to a sunless sea.

In the roaring of the waters, Kubla Khan can hear the voices of his ancestors. They prophesy war:

> And 'mid this tumult Kubla heard from far
> Ancestral voices prophesying war![11]

A war of cultures? A hyperculture without centre, without a God, without sites will continue to trigger resistance. There are many for whom it means the trauma of loss. Re-theologization, re-mythologization and re-nationalization are common reactions to the hyperculturalization of the world. Thus, hypercultural de-siting will have to confront a fundamentalism of sites. Will those 'ancestral voices' prophesying disaster be proved right? Or are they just the voices of a few revenants who will soon drift away again?

The Eros of Interconnectedness

In a posthumously published fragment, '*Die Zeit beden-ken*' [Thinking of Time], Vilém Flusser reflects on the temporality that characterizes the information society.[1] He distinguishes between three forms of time: the time of the image, the time of the book and the time of the bit – in geometrical terms, plane-like time, linear time and point-like time. The time of the image belongs to mythical time. Mythical time is a perspicuous order in which every thing has its fixed place. If something moves away from its place, it is put back. The time of the book belongs to historical time. Historical time is the linearity of history. It is a stream flowing from the past into the future. All events point towards either progress or decay. Today's time, by contrast, possesses neither a mythical nor a historical horizon. It lacks any comprehensive hori-zon of meaning. It is de-theologized, or de-teleologicized,

11

into an 'atom-like' 'universe of bits', a 'mosaic universe' in which possibilities 'buzz' like points, or 'sprinkle' like 'grains', as 'discrete sensations':

> These possibilities advance towards me: they are the future. Wherever I happen to look, there is the future. ... Put differently: the void that I am is not passive, but like a vortex it sucks in all the possibilities that surround it.

In this 'universe of points', there are no 'images', no 'books' to limit the possibilities. Rather, Dasein is surrounded by freely hovering possibilities. In this way, the 'universe of points' promises greater freedom. After all, the future is 'everywhere' that I 'turn to'.

The possibilities increase, Flusser continues, if I include others in my own time, that is, if I 'acknowledge' and 'love': 'I am not alone in the world; there are also others in it. ... By putting my own future at the disposal of the other I have the other's future at my disposal.' Perhaps Flusser would also understand interconnectedness as a practice of love and acknowledgement, for interconnectedness expands the future by creating a hyperspace of possibilities. The fundamental traits of the Dasein that inhabits this hypercultural universe would be not 'fear' and 'isolation' but Eros and interconnectedness.

The increasing interconnectedness of the world, whether it is driven by 'Eros' or by some altogether different human inclination, creates an abundance, even an overabundance, of relations and possibilities. The saturated space of possibilities, the hyperspace of possible options, exceeds the 'facticity' which would otherwise limit the 'projection', the freedom of choice, to speak with Heidegger, to 'the possibility it has inherited': 'The resoluteness in which Dasein comes back to itself, discloses current factical possibilities of authentic existing, and discloses them *in terms of the heritage* which that resoluteness, as thrown, *takes over.*'[2] 'Thrownness' is surely not one of the traits of today's human existence. Contemporary existence corresponds rather to 'being projected'. The excess of possibilities enables a projection of Dasein beyond the horizon of 'inheritance' and 'tradition'. Excess therefore has a de-facticizing effect, which leads to an increase in freedom. 'Dasein' is de-facticized into a *homo liber*. Microsoft's famous slogan 'Where do you want to go today?' encodes the de-facticization of Dasein, which dis-inherits Dasein and makes it into a hypercultural tourist. Today's culture is characterized by de-facticization. De-facticization releases Dasein from its 'thrownness' and thereby increases its freedom.

'Hypercultural tourist' is another name for de-facticized Dasein. Being a tourist does not necessarily mean being physically on the move. *Already at home*, the hypercultural tourist is either somewhere else or on the go. It is not that we leave our houses as tourists in order to return later as natives. The hypercultural tourist is *already* a tourist when *at home*. Still here, he is already there. He never *arrives* at a final destination.

The Heidegger of *Being and Time* was already convinced that all interconnecting media level out differences and produce a 'dictatorship of the "they"'. As he put it in *Being and Time*:

In utilizing public means of transport and in making use of information services such as the newspaper, every Other is like the next. This Being-with-one-another dissolves one's own Dasein completely into the kind of Being of 'the Others', in such a way, indeed, that the Others, as distinguishable and explicit, vanish more and more.[3]

The idea that media may bring about a multiplication of forms of life and possibilities is alien to Heidegger. Because he feels uneasy about diversity, he would also not want to oppose the monotony of the 'they' with a plurality of projections of Dasein. Faced with a colourful patchwork society, he would invoke the 'we' of a community of fate. Heidegger's philosophy of 'dwelling' and of the 'site' is ultimately an attempt to re-facticize Dasein.

Fusion Food

Globalization is a complex process. It does not simply lead to the disappearance of diverse signs, ideas, images, spices and smells. It is not that culture, or nature, produce either a unity or a bland homogeneous mass. Rather, the creation of difference is part of the economy of evolution, an economy that also applies to culture. Globalization proceeds dialectically; it allows dialects to emerge.

An idea of cultural plurality that took its bearings from the protection of species and could only succeed by introducing artificial enclosures would be problematic. Such a curated or ethnographic plurality would be sterile. Having lively cultural exchange means that things spread but also that certain forms of life disappear. Hyperculture is not an oversized monoculture. Through global interconnectedness and de-facticization, hyperculture provides a pool of different forms and practices of life that keeps changing, expanding and renewing itself. Under hypercultural conditions, that is, in a de-historicized form, past forms of life also enter into this pool. The spatial and temporal inclusiveness of hyperculture spells the end of 'history' in the strong sense.

Catchphrases such as 'McDonald's culture' or 'Coca-Cola culture' do not accurately reflect the actual cultural dynamic. Phenomena are projected on to McDonald's which overdetermine the meaning of the name in several ways. This projection covers up what is actually happening. There are probably more Chinese restaurants in the world than there are branches of McDonald's. Parisians probably eat more sushi than beef burgers. Modern Western cuisine is frequently influenced by Asian food. In Asia, McDonald's is no more than an occasional alternative to the native cuisine. And even McDonald's has to vary its menu in line with the eating habits of local cultures. The US is the source not just of McDonald's but also of 'fusion food', or 'fusion cuisine', an eclectic culinary approach that makes free use of all that the hypercultural pool of spices, ingredients and ways of preparing food has to offer. This hypercuisine does not level the diversity of eating cultures. It does not just blindly throw everything into one pot. Rather, it thrives on the differences. This allows it to create a diversity that would not be possible on the basis of preserving the purity of local food cultures. Globalization and diversity are not mutually exclusive.

In *The McDonaldization of Society*, George Ritzer turns McDonald's into a symbol of the rationalization of the world.[1] It may well be that imperatives of rationalization, such as efficiency, calculability and predictability, dominate many areas of life around the globe. But they will not be able to rationalize the global diversity of tastes, even of spices and smells, out of existence. Globalization is not the same thing as rationalization. Out of a fear of diversity, Plato already condemned the use of spices and the manifold dishes of Sicilian cuisine. But culture does not follow *logos*. It is more unpredictable and less logical than one might think. The pressures of unity and identity are not the driving forces of globalization. Hyperculturality has a diversifying effect.

The phenomenon of hypercuisine cannot be countered by gastronomic re-localization. The hypermarket of taste de-sites the local. This is what the local looks like in its hypercultural form: 'In short, a non-traditionalist renaissance of the local occurs . . . To put it in Bavarian and ironic terms, if it is do or die for the (veal) sausage, then the answer is a "Hawaiian toast with veal sausage".'[2]

At least as far as food is concerned, there will be no cultural homogenization. The creation of difference is part of how the sense of taste, and even enjoyment, works. The emergence of a bland cultural homogeneity would put an end to enjoyment. The levelling of differences would also not make sense in terms of the economy of consumption. The hypermarket of taste lives off difference and diversity. Hyperculturality, however, is more than a side by side of different spices and smells. It de-facticizes taste itself, opens it up to the new.

Fusion food makes you think of design rather than Being. One might even say that hyperculture de-facticizes Being into design. More than ever, life is projection. Design strips Being of its thrownness. Heidegger

17

constantly tries to re-facticize the world, including its smells, in a struggle against the world's hyperculturality. In 'The Pathway', he characteristically invokes the 'scent of the oak wood'.[3]

Hybrid Culture

The insight that culture is hybrid or impure is nothing new. According to Herder, as mentioned above, European culture is 'a plant sprung from roman, greek, and arabic feed'. It is a bastard culture. The Greek people owe their existence, Hegel said, to '*colluvies* – a conflux of the most various nations'.[1] They are, therefore, anything but pure. The 'heterogeneity in itself' that Hegel mentions in connection with the genesis of Greek culture means, in the end, the hybrid constitution of culture.

'Heterogeneity in itself' gives spirit 'the power of realizing itself as Spirit'. Seen from this perspective, spirit itself is hybrid. Without 'heterogeneity in itself', it would not possess any vitality. Hegel's identities – this is one way of reading him – are pervaded by hybrid differences. Perhaps Hegel's commitment to identity and organic unity derives from his deep insight into the hybridity of

Being. Hegel is no doubt one of the few thinkers to have approached the original dimension of 'spirit'. Originally, 'spirit' means excitation, agitation or losing one's composure. Indeed, 'spirit' is another word for 'ghost'. Etymologically, 'spirit' [*Geist*] points more towards what is uncanny [*Un-heim-lichkeit*] than towards the peace of 'being-at-home-with-oneself'. A ghost is itself a hybrid figure – half alive, half dead.

In the debates on multiculturalism, hybridity is elevated to the status of a culture-generating power that brings forth new (mixed) forms: 'Hybrid are all those things that owe their existence to a blending of lines of tradition or chains of signifiers, that connect different discourses and technologies, that are produced with the techniques of collage, sampling, bricolage.'[2]

Homi K. Bhabha's concept of hybridity questions the purity or originality of culture itself. According to him, cultures are not fixed, unchanging entities that could be the subjects of hermeneutic understanding. Hybridity marks the 'interstitial passage' that creates identity, a culture's image of itself, as an effect of differences.[3] The boundary, as a liminal space of transition, does not simply delimit or exclude; it engenders. It is an interstitial space that keeps the process of re-articulating the differences, and thus also the identities, going. Bhabha uses the metaphor of the 'stairwell': 'The hither and thither of the stairwell, the temporal movement and passage that it allows, prevents identities at either end of it from settling into primordial polarities.'[4]

As an illustration of the interstitial transition, Bhabha points to Heidegger's trope of the bridge, quoting from 'Building Dwelling Thinking': 'Always and ever differently the bridge escorts the lingering and hastening ways of men to and fro, so that they may get to other banks . . . The bridge gathers a passage that crosses.'[5] This quotation from Heidegger is incomplete and distorts the meaning. Heidegger actually says:

> Always and ever differently the bridge escorts the lingering and hastening ways of men to and fro, so that they may get to other banks and in the end, as mortals, to the other side. Now in a high arch, now in a low, the bridge vaults over glen and stream – whether mortals keep in mind this vaulting of the bridge's course or forget that they, always themselves on their way to the last bridge, are actually striving to surmount all that is common and unsound in them in order to bring themselves before the haleness of the divinities. The bridge *gathers*, as a passage that crosses, before the divinities.[6]

Heidegger's bridge is indeed, and here Bhabha is surely right, an interstitial transition that gives rise to the banks, that is, to the Here and There:

> The bridge swings over the stream 'with ease and power'. It does not just connect banks that are already there. The banks emerge as banks only as the bridge crosses the stream. The bridge designedly causes them to lie across from each other.[7]

The bridge is a symbol for the idea that, in a certain sense, the relation precedes the things it relates. For Heidegger, a relation is not a static, abstract relation between already clearly delineated entities. Rather, it

21

produces the entities in the first place. Thus, identity is the result of the dynamic of differences. Difference is not an effect that follows from identity. Heidegger emphasizes that a bridge is not simply built at an already existing site. Rather, it creates sites. It provides space and gathers. In this sense, a bridge is a 'prior casting-over' [*vorgängiger Überwurf*] within which spaces emerge.[8] And a boundary, for Heidegger – and here Bhabha quotes him correctly – 'is not that at which something stops' but that 'from which something *begins its presencing*'.[9]

Heidegger's trope of the bridge or the boundary, however, is not at all suitable as an illustration of the hybridity of culture or of the world. In Heidegger, Here and There, inside and outside, one's own and what is foreign, stand in a relation of *dialectical, dialogical* tension. Heidegger's world is determined by a strict symmetry that prevents any hybridity which would create asymmetrical entities. Dialectics, which for Heidegger take the form of dialectics without middle ground, that is, without 'reconciliation', do not permit any hybridization of what is different. The hybrid buzzing of voices which penetrate each other, mix with each other and multiply is alien to Heidegger. Its dialectical arch makes Heidegger's bridge too narrow, so to speak. It is not a wide crossing, not a square, not a *circus*[10] where, without any dialectic being involved, things could come across each other, reflect each other and blend. Bhabha's stairwell is also narrow, for his hither and thither only know 'upper and lower'.

Heidegger's bridge '*gathers*'. His is a trope of gathering and assembly. The kind of dispersal that hybridity requires does not take place within the antagonistic ten-

22

sion between Here and There. If in acoustic terms we can refer to the hybrid as *noise*, then Heidegger's world would be silent. Heidegger's bridge gathers, and also assembles all paths 'before the divinities'. The divinities Bhabha tellingly leaves out when he quotes Heidegger. The divine There, the divine bank, transcends the common and perhaps calamitous 'hither and thither' of the mortals. For Heidegger, this human 'hither and thither' would already constitute dispersal. Its movement is arrested, so to speak, by the 'haleness of the divinities'. Heidegger's bridge is ultimately a *theological* trope. His theologization of the world, in particular, prevents hybridization, while radically reducing diversity. Thus, its effect is a de-hybridizing one. Heidegger's 'things' are anything but hybrid. It is worth remembering that he remained a philosopher of 'authenticity', of 'genuineness', of 'origin' and 'essence'.

The way Bhabha thinks is still too dialectical. Dialectics does not simply mean contradiction and reconciliation. What dialectical means, most of all, is the antagonistic tension between different things. It is this dialectical, that is, antagonistic or agonal, tension that does not permit any playful kind of diversity. Even the interstitial space into which the boundary is transformed by Bhabha is still dialectical insofar as it is dominated by antagonism. Thus, Bhabha is still in thrall to the agonal-dialectical tension between colonizer and colonized, between ruler and ruled, between master and slave.

According to Bhabha, hybridity means above all else that the voice of the other, the foreigner, is always already present in what is one's own.[11] The attempt to construct an identity that is self-identical and pure, therefore, is a reflection, to speak with Herder, of a deafness or a refusal to hear the voice of the other. Bhabha's conception of hybridity opposes this construction of purity and origin, which is a phenomenon of power. Making the voice of the other audible thus subverts existing power relations. Hybridity 'reverses the effects of the colonialist disavowal, so that other "denied" knowledges enter upon the dominant discourse and estrange the basis of its authority'.[12] Bhabha grants hybridity a subversive force that is directed against the established regime of power.

On the basis of its conceptual history alone, however, hybridity is tied too fast to the racist and colonial complex of power, domination, repression and resistance, to the geometry of centre and periphery and above and below,[13] to capture the dimension of the playful that is free of this complex and thus leaves behind the dialectical, interstitial space of master and slave altogether. Hyperculture is certainly not a power-free space. But what is specific about the world of hyperculture is the expansion of spaces that can be accessed not according to an economy of power but according to aesthetic principles, that is, spaces that are part of the realm of play and semblance, which Schiller juxtaposes with the realm of force and the realm of law:

> In the midst of the awful realm of force, in the midst of the divine realm of law, the aesthetic impulse to form constructs unnoticed a third happy realm of play and of semblance in which the fetters of all circumstance are taken from man, releasing him from everything that could be called either moral or physical constraint.[14]

This realm of play and semblance, which would also differ from the realm of power, promises more freedom. Its fundamental law is, according to Schiller, 'to give freedom by means of freedom'.[15] This realm would thus be populated by *homines liberi et hilari*.

The Hyphenization of Culture

One pressing task for the philosophy of culture is to develop a model that is able to capture today's cultural dynamic. Although Bhabha's concept of hybrid 'interstitial space' goes some way to liquefying the essentialist concept of culture, it is still too rigid, too dialectical, for a description of contemporary cultural, even hypercultural, processes.

According to Bhabha, cultural identity is not the passive representation of given cultural traits. Rather, cultural identity is constantly 'negotiated' in an 'antagonistic', 'conflict-laden' interstitial space. On the notion of 'negotiation', Bhabha writes:

> When I talk of negotiation rather than negation, it is to convey a temporality that makes it possible to conceive of the articulation of antagonistic or contradictory

elements: a dialectic without the emergence of a teleological or transcendent History . . .[1]

Bhabha's model of the interstitial space does not correspond to the hypercultural side by side of what is different, which is not determined by an 'either/or' but by an 'as well as', not by contradiction or antagonism but by mutual appropriation.

Hyperculture is more open and less dialectical than Bhabha's hybrid culture. Neither the model of the bridge nor that of the stairwell or the negotiation table does justice to it. Deleuze and Guattari's model of the rhizome, by contrast, proves suitable for the description of certain aspects of hyperculture. It does have potential as a tool of cultural theory.

The 'rhizome' denotes a non-centred plurality that cannot be subjected to any comprehensive order:

A rhizome as subterranean stem is absolutely different from roots and radicles. Bulbs and tubers are rhizomes. Plants with roots or radicles may be rhizomorphic in other respects altogether: the question is whether plant life in its specificity is not entirely rhizomatic. . . . [A]ny point of a rhizome can be connected to anything other, and must be. This is very different from the tree or root, which plots a point, fixes an order.[2]

Thus, a rhizome is an open structure whose heterogeneous elements constantly play into each other, shift across each other and are in a process of permanent 'becoming'. The rhizomatic space is a space not of 'negotiation' but of transformation and blending. Rhizomatic distribution, even dispersal, de-substantializes and de-internalizes culture and thereby turns it into hyperculture.

Deleuze and Guattari sketch a rhizomatic relationship between an orchid and a wasp:

> The orchid deterritorializes by forming an image, a tracing of a wasp; but the wasp reterritorializes on that image. The wasp is nevertheless deterritorialized, becoming a piece in the orchid's reproductive apparatus. But it reterritorializes the orchid by transporting its pollen.[3]

This relationship between orchid and wasp is only apparently governed by 'mimicry'. What is actually going on is a 'veritable becoming, a becoming-wasp of the orchid and a becoming-orchid of the wasp'.[4]

Despite its intense dispersal, a rhizome also forms tree-like and root-like structures. And, in the same way, branches or parts of a root suddenly sprout rhizome-like buds.[5] As a de-internalized, de-rooted, de-sited culture, hyperculture behaves in a rhizomatic fashion. There are rhizomatic transitions between sub-cultural and cultural structures, between the peripheries and centres, between temporary concentrations and renewed dispersals. This may also lead to the formation of dominant cultural structures that resemble the knots or bulbs in a rhizomatic net. But these disperse and dissolve again. National culture, as a tree-like and root-like culture, would correspond to a covering up or conjuring away of the rhizomatic structures. Hyperculture is a rhizomatic structure. The rhizomatic proliferation and spread reflect the *hyper* (hyperculturality), and they cannot be captured by the *inter* (interculturality) or the *trans* (transculturality).

A rhizome has no 'memory'.[6] It is *scattered*, so to speak. This is another feature of rhizomatic culture that resembles hyperculture, which is not a culture of inwardness or remembrance. A botanical description of a rhizome tellingly ends with the following remark:

> The oldest parts of the rootstock always die off to the degree that its top is rejuvenated. This is also the reason why, unlike other perennial parts of a stalk, it does not continually reach larger dimensions; it only becomes another one.[7]

The Heideggerian and Bhabhaian trope of the 'bridge' that 'swings over the stream' as the banks 'lie across from each other' is anything but rhizomatic. The rhizomatic middle is not an antagonistic transition. It flees or flows too fast, so to speak, for a 'negotiation' to take place. According to Deleuze and Guattari, '*Between* things does not designate a localizable relation going from one thing to the other and back again, but a perpendicular direction, a transversal movement that sweeps one *and* the other away.' It is thus not an 'interstitial passage' but 'a stream without beginning or end that undermines its banks and picks up speed in the middle'.[8] The rhizomatic in-between is not antagonistic. It is structured by conjunction, not contradiction. It can therefore be much friendlier than Bhabha's interstitial space, which is always 'conflict-laden'. A rhizome is neither enclosing nor excluding:

> A rhizome has no beginning or end; it is . . . interbeing, *intermezzo*. The tree is filiation, but the rhizome is

alliance, uniquely alliance. The tree imposes the verb 'to be', but the fabric of the rhizome is the conjunction, 'and . . . and . . . and . . .'. This conjunction carries enough force to shake and uproot the verb 'to be'.[9]

This rhizomatic, non-dialectical, even *friendly And* deserves a lot of attention. The rhizomatic 'logic of the AND' generates a 'nonsignifying' connection, that is, a connection of the unconnected, a side by side of what is different, a closeness of what is distant.[10] It *hyphenates* culture,[11] turning it into hyperculture.[12] A hyphen connects, reconciles, even without any 'deeper' or 'inner' connection.

Hyphae, incidentally, is also the name of fungal filaments. Originally, hyphen (Greek: *hyphé*) means woven. It is a net, a *web*. By fusion, hyphae form a net-like mesh (*mycelium*). The mesh of hyphae has no centre. It is not properly *rooted*. It can only spread around or grow into the air (aerial hyphae). Under certain conditions a mesh can produce generative hyphae. It possesses little inwardness. It is de-sited. In many respects, a hyperculture is a *hyphen-culture*.

The Age of Comparison

Nietzsche was certainly one of the few thinkers capable of looking far ahead, of resonating with vibrations that came from the future. Apparently, he recognized that the death of God also presaged the end of the *site* as something of particular significance, that God was also the God of *sites*. The de-siting of culture creates a side by side of different forms of knowledge, thinking, living and believing:

> *Age of comparison.* – The less men are bound by tradition, the greater is the fermentation of motivations within them, and the greater in consequence their outward restlessness, their mingling together with one another, the polyphony of their endeavours. Who is there who now still feels a strong compulsion to attach himself and his posterity to a particular place? Who is there who still feels any strong attachment at all? Just as in the

arts all the genres are imitated *side by side*, so are all the stages and genres of morality, custom, culture. – Such an age acquires its significance through the fact that in it the various different philosophies of life, customs, cultures can be compared and experienced side by side; which in earlier ages, when, just as all artistic genres were attached to a particular place and time, so every culture still enjoyed only a localized domination, was not possible.[1]

Nietzsche had in mind a philosophy of comparing, even a *comparative philosophy*:

I imagine future thinkers in which the European-American restlessness is united with the hundredfold inherited Asian tranquillity: such a combination will solve the riddle of the world. Meanwhile, the contemplative free spirits have their mission: they lift all the barriers that stand in the way of the merging of people: religion, states, monarchical instincts, illusions of wealth and poverty, prejudices concerning health and race – etc.[2]

The age of the site becomes unbound and turns into the age of comparison. The age that is now approaching, however, rises above both the culture of the site and the culture of comparison:

Now an enhanced aesthetic sensibility will come to a definitive decision between all these forms offering themselves for comparison: most of them – namely all those rejected by this sensibility – it will allow to die out.

There is likewise now taking place a selecting out among the forms and customs of higher morality whose objective can only be the elimination of the lower moralities. This is the age of comparison! It is the source of its pride – but, as is only reasonable, also of its suffering. Let us not be afraid of this suffering! Let us rather confront the task which the age sets us as boldly as we can: and then posterity will bless us for it – a posterity that will know itself to be as much beyond the self-enclosed original national cultures as it is beyond the culture of comparison, but will look back upon both species of culture as upon venerable antiquities.[3]

Thus, the age of comparison is more than just a side by side of different cultural forms. It is an age of selection that takes its bearings from a hierarchy of values. 'Lower' moralities are supposed to die out in favour of a 'higher morality'. The only decisive criterion is 'aesthetic sensibility'. The problem, however, is how the distinction between lower and higher forms should be drawn, for instance with regard to artistic 'genres'. Nietzsche's aestheticism tends towards a re-teleologization, a re-theologization, of culture.

Will the age of globalization really have been an age of comparison that disappeared to be replaced by an age characterized by stronger, higher forms? Or will it remain an age of plurality that continues to practise an 'as well as', an age that is not dominated by the economy of selection but by the 'logic of the AND'? Will the 'higher' morality of the future, assuming it comes to exist, not precisely rest on the *friendliness of the AND*?

The De-Auratization of Culture

In post-Biblical times, God is called '*site*'.

Peter Handke[1]

Perhaps unconsciously, or pre-consciously, Microsoft's slogan 'Where do you want to go today?' registers a seismic shift in Being. 'Go' marks an incision, the end of a specific *Here*. The Linux slogan 'Where do you want to go tomorrow?' and Disney's advertising slogan on its internet portal 'Go' – 'Are you ready to go?' – similarly bid farewell to a *Here* that used to give Being its auratic depth, or rather the *semblance* of an aura.

Walter Benjamin, in his *The Work of Art in the Age of Its Technological Reproducibility*, derives the aura of a natural or artificial object from its 'unique existence in a particular place'. The aura is the resplendence and radiance of a specific 'here and now' that cannot be repeated *there*.[2] If

34

the site were the 'tip of the spear' which gathers every-thing into itself, the aura would be the expression of the site's *inwardness*.[3]

Today's globalization is *more* than just exchange between sites. Certain cultural forms moving from one site to another, one site culturally influencing another, is not yet globalization. Contemporary globalization effects a change in the site as such. It de-internalizes it, takes away the 'tip' which *gives the site its soul*. When, in the process of de-siting, cultural forms of expression detach themselves from their original sites and join together, putting themselves on offer in a hypercultural simultaneity in which the here and now gives way to site-less repetition, aura deteriorates. Culture in the age of its global reproducibility is not a culture of an auratic here and now. But the de-auratization of the site should not be lamented, in a one-sided fashion, as a loss of 'depth', 'origin', 'essence' or 'authenticity', not to mention as a loss of Being, as Heidegger's critique of culture would have it. If anything, hypercultural sitelessness is another shape of Being. And might, in the end, depth and origin even be a specific effect of the surface?[4]

According to Benjamin, aura is the 'unique appari-tion of a distance'. The decay of the aura is the result of *'the desire of the present-day masses to "get closer" to things'*.[5] The disappearance of the aura can be derived from the human aspiration to take hold of things by way of a de-distancing [*Ent-Fernung*]. Why condemn this production of nearness? Could the aura not be a semblance of beauty produced by an unhappy consciousness painfully aware that things are still lingering in the distance?

De-siting and de-distancing cause each other. Sites

are de-*distanced*. De-siting produces nearness. Cultural forms of expression are de-*distanced* by being removed from their historical or ritual context and placed side by side. They form a gapless sequence in a hypercultural space. Under conditions of hyperculture, different forms or styles from different sites and ages are de-distanced in a hyper-present. This hypercultural side by side extinguishes the aura, which emanates from a specific *Here*, from unique *sites* and specific times. Thus, globalization de-auratizes culture and turns it into hyperculture.

De-auratization is also de-facticization. Cultures become detached from their spatial-historical *embeddedness*, even their *thrownness*. As de-facticized cultures, they are open to different kinds of appropriation. De-sited, de-auratized cultures are not merely replications devoid of any authenticity. They achieve *another* Being, *another* reality, which shines in the absence of the auratic. On the model of the term hyperculturality, it could be called *hyperreality*.

William Randolph Hearst's Xanadu-like castle near San Simeon in California, now a museum, is perhaps a site of hyperreality, a site of sitelessness. Cultural goods from all over the world, of all ages, styles and traditions, are condensed into a side by side. Forgeries seamlessly combine with genuine articles, thus sublating fake and genuine into a third category of Being, into *hyperreality*. Could Hearst's 'Xanadu' be a miniature museum of hyperreality, an anticipation of global hyperreality? In a strange way, Hearst's hyperreal 'Xanadu' oddly resembles Nelson's hypertextual 'Xanadu'. In both, the world is dominated by a dense side by side, a simultaneity of what is different. The nearness of what is different or what is distant is also typical of hyperculture. Is the promise of a *more* characteristic of both the hypercultural side by side and the hypertextual or hyperreal Xanadu project?

Umberto Eco, in his essay 'Travels in Hyperreality', accuses Hearst of 'bringing the past down to the level of today's life' and criticizes his 'continuum of styles'. His 'Xanadu', Eco writes, is a 'masterpiece of bricolage, haunted by *horror vacui*'.[6] But didn't Hearst simply follow that '*desire*' to "'*get closer*" to *things*'? Hyperculturality throws a special light on Hearst's hyperreality, on the side by side of sites and ages in the absence of the auratic. Hearst's continuum of styles and bricolage resemble the hypercultural logic of the AND. Hearst's 'Xanadu' near San Simeon is, incidentally, like Disneyland, part of California's touristic landscape.

Should we lament the loss of aura, of the site, or origin, of the auratizing 'here and now'? Or does, across all these losses, a new, aura-free here and now announce itself, a here and now that nevertheless has its own splendour, a hypercultural *being-here* that coincides with *being-every-where*? Do Disney's advertising slogan 'Are you ready to go?' and Microsoft's slogan 'Where do you want to go today?' point towards the form of existence of a future *homo liber*, that is, towards the freedom that human beings might receive in return for the decay of the aura? When the 'here and now' becomes a *repeatable there* and *later*, will we have gained something or lost something?

Pilgrims and Tourists

At last, in my dream, I was the pilgrim again: that is, everything was marked by painful-sobering futility. And in the morning, upon awakening, I wanted this winter to last forever.

Peter Handke[1]

For Zygmunt Bauman, the modern human is a pilgrim. Modernity, Bauman says, gave the pilgrim 'a seminally novel twist'.[2] Modern humans, as pilgrims, walk across a desert-like earth, giving 'form to the formless', lending 'continuity to the episodic' and making 'a whole out of the fragmentary'.[3] According to Bauman, the modern pilgrimage is a 'living-towards-projects'. It is 'directional, continuous, and unbendable'.[4] Because of its nature as a project, the world of the pilgrim 'must be orderly, determined, predictable, insured'. It must be a world 'in which footprints are engraved for good, so that the trace and the record of past travels are kept and preserved'.[5]

Are modern humans really pilgrims? Does the figure of the pilgrim really correspond to modernity? The feeling that one is a stranger on this earth is a necessary ingredient in the experience of a pilgrim. A pilgrim is a *peregrinus*. He or she is not fully at home *Here*, and thus pilgrims are *on their way* to a special *There*. Modernity overcomes precisely this asymmetry between *Here* and *There*, and it thereby overcomes the form of existence of the pilgrim. Instead of being on its way towards a *There*, modernity *progresses* towards a better *Here*. But a necessary part of the pilgrim's wandering across the desert is uncertainty and insecurity, that is, the possibility of going astray. Modernity, by contrast, thinks that it is moving along a straight road.

The pilgrimage is a *pre-modern* trope. Thus it is a trope that re-theologizing thinkers like Heidegger fall back on. Part of 'Being' is 'straying' [*Irren*].[6] Heidegger's 'on the way to' has the structure of a pilgrimage. The desire for a *definitive arrival*, a home, is inherent in it. The 'on the way to' is, after all, tied to that 'origin' which is not available in the visible Here. Heidegger's 'Pathway' was a pilgrim's route. Also characteristic of a pilgrimage is the 'need/of hesitant darkness/in the waiting light'.[7] Pilgrims' routes are the 'arduously long paths/into the ever simpler, the naïvity/of the site-ness/that is denied us in the inaccessible'.[8] This denial is what re-auratizes and re-theologizes the 'site-ness'.

In some respects, the first tourists still had the gait of pilgrims. They were on their way towards a romantic counter-world, a primitive and untouched place. They wanted to escape from a *Here* to a *There*. But even then the tourist was no longer a *peregrinus*, not a stranger or a wanderer (*viator*). The tourist had a *home*, a *being-at-home in the Here*.

Hyperculturality creates a particular kind of tourist. Hypercultural tourists are not on their way to a counter-world, to a *There*. They rather inhabit a space that does not contain an asymmetry between *Here* and *There*. They are *fully here*. They are *at home in a space of immanence*. Surfing or browsing in the hyperspace of attractions is decisively different from the gait of the pilgrim, as well as that of the romantic tourist. In the space of hyperculture, *There* is only another *Here*. It is symmetrical. There is no asymmetry of pain. The hypercultural tourist moves from one *Here* to another *Here*. Hyperculture is a *culture of Being-Here*. Because a hypercultural tourist does not seek a definitive arrival, the place where he or she happens to be is not a *site*, not a *Here* in the strong sense. Thus, in the context of hyperculture, the Here should either be lower cased or struck through: Here. As opposed to the crossed-out Being in Heidegger, who intends to re-auraticize and re-theologize Being, the simple strikethrough of the Here points towards the de-auratization and de-theologization of Being. It takes away Being's auratic depth.

Although Zygmunt Bauman remarks, apropos of the tourist, that 'it is less and less clear which one of the visiting places is the home, and which but a tourist haunt', he nevertheless holds on to the trope of the home:

> The opposition 'here I am but visiting, there is my home' stays clear cut as before, but it is not easy to point out where the 'there' is. 'There' is increasingly stripped of all material features; the 'home' it contains

is not even *imaginary* (any mental image would be too specific, too constraining) – but *postulated*; what is postulated is *having* a home, not a particular building, street, landscape or company of people. . . . Homesickness is a *dream of belonging* – of being for once, *of* the place, not merely *in*. . . . The value of 'home' in the homesickness lies precisely in its tendency to stay in the future tense forever. It cannot move to the present without being stripped of its charm and allure.[9]

Bauman's tourists are romantic tourists who postulate a counter-world. They are still pilgrims. They are on their way towards a home, to a There, which, however, retreats into the 'future tense'. Bauman adds that homesickness 'is not the sole tourist's sentiment', that tourists also know the 'fear of *home-boundedness*', that is, 'of being tied to a place'.[10] But Bauman does not recognize an altogether different kind of tourist, that is, the form of existence of the hypercultural tourist, who, in contrast to the pilgrim tourist, knows of no difference between Here and There, who therefore does not live in the 'future tense' or in 'future II' but fully in the *present tense*, who fully inhabits the space of *Being-Here*. For Bauman, tourists are still pilgrims torn between the longing for the There and their fear of it. A hypercultural tourist knows neither longing nor fear.

Globalization does not simply mean that the There is connected with the Here. Rather, it creates a global Here by de-distancing and de-siting the There. This global Here cannot be grasped on the basis of the concepts of inter-, multi- or trans-culturality. Hypercultural tourists travel in the hyperspace of events, a space of *cultural sightseeing*. In this way, they experience culture as cul-tour.

Windows and Monads

Ted Nelson conceives of the idea of the hypertext as an exercise in freedom. The hypertext can be interpreted as a symbol for general emancipation. According to Nelson, the production of a linear-hierarchical order is based on compulsion, on a 'destructive process'.[1] The reader of a conventional book is forced to submit to the pre-given order. Thus, the book does not do justice to the different preferences of different readers:

> People have different backgrounds and styles . . . Yet sequential text, to which we are funnelled by tradition and technology, forces us to write the same sequences for everyone, which may be appropriate for some readers and leave others out in the cold, or which may be appropriate for nobody.[2]

The reader is forced into passivity. Hypertext, by contrast, allows the reader to adopt an altogether different attitude. It provides the possibility of choice:

> Thus it would be greatly preferable if we could easily create different pathways for different readers, based upon background, taste and probably understanding . . . This means that 'different' articles and books will more likely be *different versions of the same work, and different pathways through it for different readers.*[3]

The hypertextual world is 'colored'.[4] The reader is no longer thrown into a monochrome structure of meaning and order. Rather, the reader moves actively, lays pathways through the multicoloured space of the hypertext. He or she is a tourist in a colourful hyperspace. Nelson speaks of 'active reading'.[5] The reader follows not so much a pre-given order but his or her own inclinations and interests:

> Unrestricted by sequence, in hypertext we may create new forms of writing which better reflect the structure of what we are writing *about*; and readers, choosing a pathway, may follow their interests or current line of thought in a way heretofore considered impossible.[6]

The world is a kind of 'windowing hypertext'.[7] Windows give access to a hypertextual universe. Experience of the world consists of a '*step through* the window':

> Think of the present document as a sheet of glass. It may have writing painted on it by the present author; it

may have clear glass, windowing to something else; the next pane may be in turn made of more layers of painted glass, with more windows, and so on indefinitely.[8]

Windowing is thus the hypertextual mode of experience. It opens up the world. In this hypertextual universe there are no longer any isolated units; thus there are no longer any 'subjects'. Each person mirrors every other, or allows others to shine through them.

The hypertextual universe contrasts in an interesting way with Leibniz's universe, because the inhabitants of that universe, the monads, have no windows at all. A monad reflects the universe within itself, but this reflection is an inner reflection, as the monad is 'windowless'. And the reason for this is that the monad is a 'substance': it is closed to all sides; it rests in itself. Thus, Leibniz's monadic universe is not a net universe. As the monads are windowless, no *windowing* takes place in this universe. The closed nature of the monadic 'substance' does not permit any communication, and thus no mutual mirroring. This is where, famously, Leibniz's 'God' comes into the equation. God mediates between the windowless monads and guarantees the 'prestabilized harmony' between the isolated monads.

In the hypertextual universe, nothing is monadically closed, for in it there are no 'subjects'. The inhabitant of a hypertextual universe would be a kind of window creature, consisting of windows through which it receives the world. *Windowing* robs the house of its monadic inwardness, de-internalizing its inhabitant, who thus becomes a hypercultural tourist.

A window actually has two functions. To begin with, it

44

is an opening to the outside. But it also seals me off against the world. The screen, too, as a kind of window, reveals as well as shields. *Windowing* can therefore also produce monads, this time monads with windows whose Being-in-the-world turns out to be a Being-before-a-window. In their isolation they come close to the old windowless monads. Will they also have to call on *God*?

Odradek

Kafka's creature 'Odradek', in *The Cares of a Family Man*, embodies a hybrid identity.[1] Even his name indicates hybridity: 'Some say the word Odradek is of Slavonian origin, and try to account for it on that basis. Others again believe it to be of German origin, only influenced by Slavonic.'[2] His appearance is also hybrid:

> At first glance it looks like a flat star-shaped spool for thread, and indeed it does seem to have thread wound upon it; to be sure, they are only old, broken-off bits of thread, knotted and tangled together, of the most varied sorts and colors. But it is not only a spool, for a small wooden crossbar sticks out of the middle of the star, and another small rod is joined to that at a right angle. By means of this latter rod on one side and one of the points of the star on the other, the whole thing can stand upright as if on two legs.[3]

Most of all, Odradek is hybrid because he does not observe the boundaries of the 'house'. He is a counter-figure to the house or site. He has no attachment to any site. He therefore constantly irritates the '*Hausvater*', the father of the house, this guardian of the home, the nation, the fatherland or the people. He is the care of the 'father of the house'. Like a ghost, with no fixed abode, Odradek haunts the spaces of the house:

> He lurks in turns in the garret, the stairway, the lobbies, the entrance hall. Often for months on end he is not to be seen; then he has presumably moved into other houses; but he always comes faithfully back to our house again.[4]

You cannot help, the father says, but approach Odradek 'like a child'; you 'put no difficult questions to him'. Odradek is clearly not a deep thinker. He has no strong attachments to things or sites: '"Well, what's your name?" you ask him. "Odradek" he says. "And where do you live?" "No fixed abode", he says and laughs.' Odradek's identity is very odd:

> One is tempted to believe that the creature once had some sort of intelligible shape and is now only a broken-down remnant. Yet this does not seem to be the case; at least there is no sign of it; nowhere is there an unfinished or unbroken surface to suggest anything of the kind; the whole thing looks senseless enough, but in its own way perfectly finished. In any case, closer scrutiny is impossible, since Odradek is extraordinarily nimble and can never be laid hold of.[5]

Odradek's identity is not controlled by any teleology. He looks broken only because he is not part of any purposive horizon. Despite this 'senseless' appearance, he possesses an identity, for he is in his 'own way perfectly finished'. But it is an identity that is *cobbled together* from various parts. His identity is characterized by a being-together of what is as such unconnected.

Odradek 'laughs'. But his laugh has something ironic, mocking or uncanny about it. It is not a free laughter: 'it is only the kind of laughter that has no lungs behind it. It sounds rather like the rustling of fallen leaves.' The serenity that might be ascribed to Odradek, even to Kafka himself, is as ambivalent as this disembodied laughter. Odradek's laughter is only a short interruption of the unfathomable muteness of physical matter, into which he slips again and again: 'often he stays mute for a long time, like the wood that he appears to be'.[6]

Odradek represents a kind of anti-father or anti-house. He resembles the 'nomads from the North' in *An Old Manuscript*. This story also begins with the confession of a 'care' [*Sorge*]:

> It looks as if much had been neglected in our country's [*Vaterland*] system of defense. We have not concerned ourselves with it until now and have gone about our daily work; but things that have been happening recently begin to trouble us [*machen uns aber Sorgen*].[7]

The nomads from the North have conquered the capital. They 'camp under the open sky, for they abominate dwelling houses'.[8] Like Odradek, they are not residents of a house. Again the figure of the 'father' appears, this time in the form of the 'fatherland' and 'Emperor'. As in Odradek's case, the father of the house, that is, the 'Emperor', can only look on helplessly as events unfold. The 'nomads from the North' represent the wholly other, the foreign, the uncanny, the incommensurable:

> They often make grimaces; then the whites of their eyes turn up and foam gathers on their lips, but they do not mean anything by that, not even a threat; they do it because it is their nature to do it.[9]

There is no exchange or communication between the nomads and the native citizens: 'Speech with the nomads is impossible. They do not know our language, indeed they hardly have a language of their own.' Nor do they understand 'sign language'.[10] Thus, they communicate 'much as jackdaws do', by screeching.

Neither Odradek nor the nomads from the North are hypercultural tourists. Odradek 'always comes faithfully back' to his 'house'. The trope of *windowing* is nowhere to be found in Kafka. The negativity of Kafka's nomadism only produces ghosts that haunt the *house*. Kafka thus remains a hostage of the 'house' or the 'father'. However, Odradek's hybrid nature, which, compared to the nomads' bestial nature, at least exhibits some friendly or serene traits, does somewhat resemble the patchwork structure of hypercultural identity. Odradek, Kafka tells us, consists of 'bits of thread, knotted and tangled together, of the most varied sorts and colors'. Thus, he has a *coloured Self*.[11]

Hypercultural Identity

In Leibniz's universe, every being has a fixed place and a fixed identity. It is a universe embedded in a divine harmony, in a cosmic order. Nothing can trouble it. Nothing alien penetrates its orderly inwardness. Thus, none of the monads looks out of a window.

Our present age is characterized by the collapse of horizons. Contexts that provide meaning and identity are disappearing, and the symptomatic results are fragmentation, a kind of pointillism, and pluralization. This also applies to the way we experience time. There is no longer the sort of fulfilling time that is due to a beautiful structure of past, present and future, that is, to a story, to narrative suspense. Time becomes *naked*, that is, devoid of narration. A point-like time, or event time, emerges. Because it is poor in horizons, this kind of time is not able to carry much *meaning*.

Today's constellation of Being seems to lack the gravitational centres that would unite parts into a binding totality. Being dissipates. It turns into a hyperspace of possibilities and events, which, instead of gravitating towards each other, only whizz around, so to speak. The decay of horizons is felt as a painful void, as a narrative crisis. But it also makes possible a new practice of freedom.

A world with a hypertextual structure consists of countless windows, so to speak, but none of the windows open on to an absolute horizon. This lack of a horizon-like anchor for Being makes possible a new way of proceeding, a new perspective. When *windowing*, you slide from one window to the next, from one possibility to another. This makes possible a personal narrative, an individual projection of Dasein [*Daseinsentwurf*]. When the horizon disintegrates into multicoloured possibilities, you can cobble together an identity from these parts. In place of a monochrome self there emerges a multicoloured self, a *coloured Self*.[1]

A so-called patchwork religion – one could also call it a multicoloured religion – presupposes the decay of a unified horizon of meaning. The decay of the horizon leads to a hypercultural side by side of different forms of faith, on the basis of which individuals can construct their own religions. A plurality of colours and forms, however, is not always a sign of vitality. In the case of religion, it may herald the end, annihilation. Art also works *additively*, helping itself to whatever it finds in the hypercultural pool of expressive forms and stylistic means. Hypercultural art no longer pursues the *truth* in the strong sense; it has nothing to *reveal*. Like patchwork religion, it presents itself as multicoloured and multiform.

Hyperculture does not produce a homogeneous, mono-chrome, uniform culture. Rather, it triggers increasing individualization. Individuals follow their own inclinations, cobbling together their identities from what they find in the hypercultural pool of practices and forms of life. In this way, patchwork structures and identities emerge. Their multicoloured nature points towards a new practice of freedom, one owed to the hypercultural de-facticization of the lifeworld.

Interculturality, Multiculturality and Transculturality

Interculturality and multiculturality are in many respects phenomena of the West. Historically, they are connected with nationalism and colonialism. Philosophically, they presuppose the introduction of an essentialist notion of culture. The idea of inter-culturality bases culture on an 'essence'. Linking culture to nationalism and ethnicity breathes a 'soul' into it. The 'inter', then, refers to a 'dialogue' between essentialist cultures. According to this understanding of culture, cultural exchange is not a process that makes culture what it is in the first place, but a special act, a cause seen as worth 'promoting'.

Interculturality functions according to the same model as intersubjectivity or interpersonality, which represent human beings as subjects and persons respectively. Multiculturality's understanding of culture does not fundamentally differ from that of interculturality. Cultural differences, which simply *happen to be* there, are dealt with through 'integration' or 'tolerance'. Multiculturality therefore offers little space for mutual penetration or reflection. Bhabha's conception of an 'interstitial transition' through which identities emerge as the effects of differences represents a first step towards a de-substantialization of cultures, but it does not lead to a hypercultural *windowing*.

This ontology of culture as substance is alien to the Far East, which does not see humans as individual totalities with clearly delineated contours, that is, as persons. The human being does not have a 'soul'. The Chinese sign for 'human being' already reveals that the human being is not taken for a substance. The word for 'human being' includes the sign for 'between'. The human being is thus a relation. Western categories such as intersubjectivity or interpersonality, which serve to establish a relation after the persons or subjects are already there, would be alien to the thinking of the Far East. *Before* any 'inter', the human being is a *between*. 'Dia-logue' is accordingly also a Western concept. The culture of the Far East does not know the eloquence of the *dia-legein*. Its distinct understanding of culture also explains why there is not even a fixed expression or consistent translation for 'interculturality' in the Far East. Instead, there are various ways of paraphrasing the term, which often sound very artificial.[1]

European culture, as well as the European concept of culture, exhibits a great deal of inwardness. By contrast, there is very little inwardness in the culture of the Far East. It is porous and open. For the same reason, it possesses a strong inclination towards adoption and change, towards the novel. The culture of the Far East is not a culture of re-membrance or of memory. Because of this intense openness, the question of an 'inter', the mediation between rigid essences, does not arise. The inner constitution of the culture of the Far East tends more strongly towards hyperculture, which is not a culture of inwardness either.

The thought of the Far East is based not on 'substance' but on 'relation'. Accordingly, it views the world as a network rather than as a 'Being'. It thinks in terms of networks. This is perhaps why networking has progressed more swiftly in the Far East than in the West: it apparently fits well with the Asian self-understanding and understanding of the world. The Far East has a very 'natural' relationship with 'technical' networking.

The Far East's perception of globalization does not correspond to 'place polygamy'.[2] In the Far East, there is at best a very small minority of people who enter into a 'marriage to several places at once'.[3] This does not mean, however, that it is not yet in the grip of globalization. Instead, in the Far East, globalization needs to be described in a different way. Nor does the concept of multiculturality capture the way in which cultural globalization has taken place there. It has not been shaped by colonialism and immigration, which are constitutive for the multiculturalism of the West. Despite the absence of multiculturalism, the Far East is increasingly developing towards hyperculturalism. Hyperculturality does not necessarily presuppose multiculturalism.

Where interculturality emphasizes the dialogical, transculturality emphasizes the 'crossing of borders': 'In the case of transcultural communication the process of crossing the border from one cultural unit to another is the focus of attention.'[4] Wolfgang Welsch's notion of transculturality also stresses the dynamic of cultural transgression: 'The term "transculturality" . . . is meant to signal that . . . today's cultural formations . . . *pass across*, transgress the classical borders between cultures as a matter of course.'[5] Unlike transculturality, hyperculturality does not involve this stress on the crossing of borders. The hypercultural is an immediate side by side of different cultural forms. In the hypercultural space, in the hypermarket of cultures, there is no 'hiking': different cultural forms, ideas, sounds and smells are offered up in a borderless hyperspace. The vastness of space, which is inherent in the notion of 'hiking', is altogether absent from hypercultural simultaneity. In the hypercultural space, one does not 'hike'; one 'browses' what is presently available. Genuine 'hiking' is not the hypercultural way of proceeding. Where everything is presently available, there is no sense of departure or arrival. The hypercultural tourist has always already arrived. He or she is neither a 'hiker' nor a 'cross-border commuter', and the hypercultural space involves no transition or transit. Hyperculture produces a singular *here*. If heterogeneous contents lie adjacent to one another, there is no need for the 'trans'. Contemporary culture is marked not by the trans, the multi or the inter but by the *hyper*. The cultures between which an inter or a trans would take place are un-bounded, de-sited, and de-distanced: they have been turned into hyper-culture.

Hypercultural *windowing* is not 'dialogue'; it does not involve dialogical inwardness. In a certain respect, hyperculture is *dispersed*. The hypercultural tourist is not a *hermeneutician*. Hyperculture also differs from multi-culture insofar as it involves little *remembrance* of origin, descent, ethnicity or site. And notwithstanding all of its dynamism, hyperculture is based on a dense side by side of different ideas, signs, symbols, images and sounds. It is a kind of cultural hypertext. This dimension of the 'hyper' is precisely what transculturality lacks. Today's culture is characterized not by the vastness of the 'trans' but by the nearness of the spatiotemporal side by side. The nature of globalization is characterized not by the 'multi' or the 'trans' but by the 'hyper' (accumulation, networking, compression).

Welsch remarks that culture – 'not only today' but always – has 'a transcultural design'.[6] Although this transculturality has apparently been active in every age and every culture, the culture of *today*, by contrast, is characterized by hyperculturality. Hyperculturality presupposes certain historical, sociocultural, technical and media processes. It is further linked to a novel experience of space and time, a type of identity formation and a form of perception. For instance, the Greek culture, Roman culture and the culture of the Renaissance were not hypercultural. Hyperculturality is a phenomenon of *today*.

Appropriation

In recent times, the paradigm of the 'Other' or the 'radically Other' has been introduced into many humanities disciplines, and since then appropriation has come to be seen as something rather sinful. The claim is that appropriation reduces the Other to the Same. Seeking to understand the Other is also suspect, because it involves forcing the Other into the categories of one's own thinking. In this way, the Other or the alien comes to be something that evades all appropriation. The boundless exploitation of the Other is followed by either the Other's mythical tabooization or the apotheosis of the Other.

Appropriation is not per se violent. Colonial exploitation, which destroys the Other in favour of itself and of the Same, must be strictly distinguished from appropriation. Appropriation is an essential part of education and identity. Only an idiot or a god could live without appropriation. What is one's own is not something that is simply given as a datum. Rather, it is the result of successful appropriation. Without appropriation, there also is no renewal. Hyperculture desires such appropriation; it enjoys the novel. It is a culture of intense appropriation.

The one who appropriates the Other does not remain the same. Appropriation leads to a transformation of one's own. Therein consists the dialectic of appropriation. Appropriation transforms not only the appropriating subject but also the appropriated Other. The process of appropriation does not perpetuate the Same. Rather, it produces difference. The Other is not perceived as 'exotic'. The exoticizing gaze consolidates that which is its own.

Hyperculture does not know the 'radically Other' that is the source of timidity or terror. The alien makes way for the novel. The alien is not part of the vocabulary of hyperculture. In place of timidity or recoil, hyperculture has curiosity. What one deems worthy of protection and seeks to exclude from any possible process of exchange becomes mere folklore. What is one's own is first appropriated from the cultural hyperspace. That means it is not inherited but acquired. The often destructive division between one's own and the alien is relaxed. It turns into the division between the old and the new. On the agenda is: being prepared for difference, for the new.

Consumption is also a practice of appropriation. Consumption is not just the greedy ingestion of the Other that leaves the consuming subject unchanged. The things we appropriate, with which we surround ourselves, create the substance of our selves in the first place. It is the myth of pure inwardness that reduces consumption to a purely external act. The criticism of consumption presupposes a deep inner self that needs to be protected against an excess of external things. This inwardness, this 'soul', is unknown in the Far East. This is also the reason why the Far East has a positive attitude towards consumption. It does not know any 'essence', any 'inwardness', that would need to be protected against too much 'outwardness'. Rather, the 'inward' is seen as a particular effect of the 'outward'.

On Lasting Peace

For Kant, the 'state of nature' is not a state of peace but a 'state of war'. Hence, peace must first be 'formally constituted'.[1] Immediately after setting out the principles of perpetual peace, such as 'cosmopolitan right' and 'hospitality',[2] Kant adds some 'supplements'. In the first of these, he invokes, surprisingly, '*Nature*'. Despite the fact that the 'state of nature' is a state of war, nature, 'the great artist', provides us with a guarantee 'of a perpetual peace'.[3]

'The idea of international law', Kant says, 'presupposes the separate existence of many independent adjoining states'. The 'amalgamation of the separate nations under a single power which has overruled the rest and created a universal monarchy' does not achieve a 'lasting peace' because it develops into 'despotism'. 'But', Kant continues, '*nature* wills it otherwise.'[4] It makes sure that the states remain separate, using two means to separate the nations and prevent them from intermingling – linguistic and *religious* differences. These may certainly occasion mutual hatred and provide pretexts for wars, but as culture grows and men gradually move towards greater agreement over their principles, they lead to mutual understanding and peace. And unlike that universal despotism which saps all man's energies . . . this peace is created and guaranteed by an equilibrium of forces and a most vigorous rivalry.[5]

Kant repeatedly invokes the 'great artist *Nature*'. Apparently, reason on its own is not capable of bringing about perpetual peace. Kant thus says that nature comes 'to the aid of the universal and rational human will, so admirable in itself but so impotent in practice'.[6] As a 'great artist', it even manages to combine things that are opposed to each other. It not only separates the states from each other but also 'unites nations . . . by means of their mutual self-interests'. What Kant has in mind here is the '*spirit of commerce*', which, according to him, is incompatible with war. This spirit ensures that wherever in the world war threatens to break out, states will intervene and mediate. The 'spirit of commerce sooner or later takes hold of every people': 'In this way, nature guarantees perpetual peace by the actual mechanism of human inclinations.'[7] According to this train of thought, the 'spirit of commerce' that pushes the process of globalization forwards may turn out to be stronger than the gods who wage war against each other in the *clash of cultures*.[8]

Just a few years earlier, Kant was still strongly condemning the 'spirit of commerce'. In the *Critique of Judgment* he says:

> Even war has something sublime about it if it is carried on in an orderly way and with respect for the sanctity of the citizens' rights. At the same time it makes the way of thinking of a people that carries it on in this way all the more sublime in proportion to the number of dangers in the face of which it courageously stood its ground. A prolonged peace, on the other hand, tends to make prevalent a mere commercial spirit, and along with it base selfishness, cowardice, and softness, and to debase the way of thinking of that people.[9]

What would actually be the difference between a 'lasting' and a 'perpetual' peace? Is the peace based on the 'spirit of commerce' a 'lasting' one and the peace that rests on 'morality' perpetual? Kant manoeuvres himself into a paradoxical situation. The 'lasting' peace that weakens 'morality' is a 'guarantee' for the 'perpetual' peace that should rest on 'morality'.

Even if it were based exclusively on the 'spirit of commerce', then, globalization would be able to bring about a 'lasting' peace. For this reason, the 'spirit of commerce', though it arises out of low 'inclinations', should still be affirmed. There is, then, not such a big difference between 'lasting' and 'perpetual' peace.

Something Kant would not have approved of, namely the blending of races, religions and languages, might also contribute to a lasting peace. This kind of mixing is detrimental to power and rule. The exercise of power presupposes continuity. In a discontinuous space, or a space that keeps changing its structure, power is hard to establish. Thus, blending troubles those forms of power which seek to construct a pure culture or race in order to stabilize or legitimize their rule.

Something similar must also have been on Nietzsche's mind when he wrote:

Trade and industry, the post and the book-trade, the possession in common of all higher culture, rapid changing of home and scene, the nomadic life now lived by all who do not own land – these circumstances are necessarily bringing with them a weakening and finally an abolition of nations ... so that as a consequence of continual crossing a mixed race ... must come into being out of them.[10]

It may be that this inclination towards blending also derives from 'nature'. What would be unnatural would be 'artificial nationalism', that is, the 'separation of nations through the production of *national* hostilities'. According to Nietzsche, 'mixing will nonetheless go slowly forward'. Nationalism 'is in its essence a forcibly imposed state of siege and self-defence inflicted on the many by the few and requires cunning, force and falsehood to maintain a front of respectability'.[11] For this reason, one should actively 'work for the amalgamation of nations'.[12] The world peace that would result would rest not on 'separation' but on an amalgamation of nations and peoples that would have no need for 'a single power which has overruled the rest and created a universal monarchy'. Nature, the 'great artist', would help this mixing on its way, even without resorting to power. In a time when, following the death of God, the *site* threatens to disappear, 'artificial nationalism' would be a kind of fundamentalism of the site. 'We who are homeless', Nietzsche says, are 'too "well-travelled"' to fall for nationalism.[13] For Nietzsche, the 'real value and meaning of the present culture' lay in a 'mutual amalgamation and fertilization'.[14]

Despite Nietzsche's remarkable far-sightedness, he could not yet have suspected what kind of culture would emerge in the wake of the 'rapid changing of home and scene'. He did not develop the idea of a hyperculture. And he did not always affirm the 'mixing of cultures'. In another place, Nietzsche says that it leads to 'much ugliness' and to a 'darkening of the world'.[15] In many respects, the effect of hyperculture is an un-bounding. In this way, it is also a culture beyond *'beautiful'* and *'ugly'*.

Culture of Friendliness

Hypercultural interconnectedness produces a dynamic diversity of forms of life and perception. It does not allow for a common horizon of experience or generally valid rules of behaviour. The mutual adaptation needed for a successful being-with must therefore be achieved in a different way.

One possible attitude towards the plurality of convictions, or, as Rorty puts it, 'final vocabularies', is an ironic stance. Rorty's 'ironist' has 'radical and continuing doubts about the final vocabulary she currently uses'. She does not adopt the erroneous opinion 'that her vocabulary is closer to reality than others, that it is in touch with a power other than herself'.[1] The 'ironists', Rorty says, are 'always aware of the contingency and fragility of their final vocabularies, and thus of their selves'.[2] They do not consider their final vocabularies to be absolute endpoints, and are always prepared to 'revise' them.[3]

The moral quality of Rorty's irony, however, goes no further than 'avoiding the humiliation of others'. Rorty believes that the 'recognition of a common susceptibility to humiliation is the *only* social bond that is needed'.[4] That is the reason why 'the liberal ironist needs as much imaginative acquaintance with alternative final vocabularies as possible, not just for her own edification, but in order to understand the actual and possible humiliation of the people who use these alternative final vocabularies'.[5]

An ironic distance from one's own final vocabulary certainly makes it possible for people to exist side by side without engaging in mutual 'humiliation'. It creates a noble self that does not insult other selves. But irony has no *networking* effect. It does not create connections or alliances. Rather, it produces a community of considerate monads who possess the skill of 'imaginative identification', that is, the 'ability to envisage . . . the actual and possible humiliation of others'.[6] The ironic monads are not *creatures of nets*, even with their sensitive feelers. The ironic culture remains a culture of monadic selves. There is much inwardness in this culture. It is therefore unable to capture the blend of cultural vocabularies that lacks this inwardness. One could also put it like this: the spices and smells that are interculturally blended, multiplied, are not ironic. Is there such a thing as an ironic sense of smell? We can only say that, at its deepest level, culture is not ironic.

Rorty's ironic culture does not capture the hypercultural constitution of today's world. The consciousness of contingency and fragility, for instance, which is characteristic of irony, does not reflect the experience of the manifold *hyper*. It may be the consciousness of modernity or postmodernity but not that of *hypermodernity*. Negativity, which, because of its conceptual genesis, irony cannot shed, is not a part of hyperculture. Hyperculture contains an affirmation that the ironic mode cannot grasp. Hyperculture is animated by something *infinite*. Given today's plurality of life forms and convictions, 'tact' is certainly very important. According to Gadamer, tact provides orientation in situations 'for which knowledge from general principles does not suffice'.[7] The 'achievement of undemonstrable tact' is 'to hit the target and to discipline the application of the universal, the moral law (Kant), in a way that reason itself cannot'.[8] Despite being concerned with the particular, tact does not represent the radically other of the general or of reason. It supplements the general, taking care of those things that the general cannot capture. Tact thereby gives the system suppleness and flexibility. Although it possesses a sensitivity for the particular, tact is only effective when combined with the application of the general and identical.

Politeness, too, accomplishes a formal external adaptation by providing a space for mutual self-presentation. It is a communicative technology that makes sure that words and acts do not cause hurt feelings. However, it is characterized by very limited openness. Politeness, after all, is often used to minimize contact with others, with their otherness. It keeps others at a distance. Moreover, politeness is bound up with a cultural code. Where differently coded cultures meet, it loses its efficacy.

Toleration also exhibits very little openness. The other, or stranger, is merely tolerated. What is tolerated is that which deviates from the expectations that are produced by a system of norms. Toleration has a stabilizing effect on fixed systems of rules. Neither toleration nor politeness is characterized by an unregulated openness towards what is other. Irony does not involve this openness either. These three are thus not *friendly*.

In a 'multicultural' society, toleration is mainly something practised by the majority, which represents normality. What is tolerated is whatever deviates from this normality, from the rule, and what constitutes minorities. In this way, toleration perpetuates the distinction between one's own and the other. It is not the majority but the minority that is tolerated, and there is something base and inferior about minorities. Toleration thus tacitly solidifies the status quo. For everyone involved, what is their own is what is decisive. There is no contact with the other beyond toleration. A form of openness in which what *lies outside* is not just 'tolerated' but actively affirmed, appropriated, lifted up and made a part of one's own is not proper to toleration. Toleration preserves what is one's own. Like politeness, it is a rather conservative concept.

Unlike politeness, friendliness acts without rules. Precisely because of this irregularity, it can have far-reaching effects. It produces maximum cohesion with minimum connectedness. Where the shared horizon disintegrates into the most diverse identities and ideas, politeness initiates a singular form of participation, a *continuum* of *discontinuities*. Within the hypercultural patchwork universe, it has a reconciling effect, making the side by side of what is different a *liveable* space. Neither irony nor politeness produces closeness. Because it involves an openness that goes far beyond that involved in toleration, friendliness is capable of that windowing which opens and connects. Perhaps friendliness takes the place of Leibniz's God, who helps the windowless monads establish a harmonious being-with. Friendliness gives the monads windows.

Hyperlogue

In a way, the World Wide Web has transformed the world into a seascape. When you clicked on the old Netscape Navigator, an image of a starlit sea and a lighthouse appeared. You navigate across the endless sea of information. Thus, you go on the World Wide Web the way you set sail. Instead of 'logging on' one could say 'embarking'. The sea, however, does not appear as threatening as it did in earlier times. For Hegel, the sea was still a symbol of frightening uncertainty and unfathomable depth. In his inaugural lecture at the University of Berlin, he compared thinking to an adventurous maritime journey on a boundless ocean:

With the decision to philosophize, mind throws itself into thinking (– thinking is alone with itself), – it throws itself *as if into an endless ocean*, all the bright colours, all footholds have disappeared, all other friendly lights are extinguished. Only the one star, mind's *inner star*, shines; it is the *North Star*. But it is natural that mind, being alone with itself, *is seized by horror, so to speak; you do not know yet whereto it will go, and where you will end up*.[1]

Hegel's system is based on this feeling of 'horror'; after all, it is erected in the middle of an 'endless ocean'. Kubla Khan's pleasure-dome, 'Xanadu', does not rest on solid ground either. The earth is seething, and the sacred river, Alph, tumbles down to a sunless sea. The World Wide Web presents an altogether different kind of sea, one neither of uncertainty nor of unfathomable depth. Indeed, surfing the internet is the very opposite of an adventurous maritime journey into uncertainty. In the World Wide Web, the user is a tourist who moves about by way of hyperlinks. Surfing reflects the feeling of a life that has long been familiar to us from the world outside of the computer. The user travels in the World Wide Market, that is, in the hypermarket of information. The sea, with its innumerable container ships, is no longer the sea of Homer or Hegel. The concept of 'browsing' draws our attention to a different form of being-in-the-world. Unlike 'surfing', 'browsing' is not a maritime image. The user does not have the attitude of the adventurous sea-farer but that of the consumer, even the tourist.

When the sea is transformed into a hypermarket, that *inner star of the mind*, which Hegel believed would help him master the unfathomable depth and uncertainty of an endless ocean, pales. This changing attitude towards the sea reflects today's altered understanding of Being.

The new seascape knows neither the mind nor logos in the strict sense. Logos gives way to hyperlogue, but the hyperlogue is not a simple continuation of the dialogue or polylogue. Rather, it altogether leaves behind the order of the old logos, to which both dialogue and polylogue are still attached. The hyperlogue is the new order of hyperculture; what resounds in the term, however, is less the logos than the 'log-in', or the 'logo' or 'logo-s'.

The Wanderer

Nietzsche believed the 'wanderer' to be a new type of human. In an aphorism titled 'The Wanderer' he says:

> He who has attained to only some degree of freedom of mind cannot feel other than a wanderer on the earth – though not as a traveller to a final destination: for this destination does not exist. But he will watch and observe and keep his eyes open to see what is really going on in the world; for this reason he may not let his heart adhere too firmly to any individual thing; within him too there must be something wandering that takes pleasure in change and transience.[1]

Nietzsche's wanderer walks about in a de-teleologized, de-theologized, that is, in a de-sited world. As he is not on the way to a 'final destination', he can for the first time *look around*. Insofar as he is not hostage to an ultimate meaning [*Sinn*], he is a *homo liber*. Etymologically, '*Sinn*' suggests a walk, path or journey. The new journey has no ultimate destination. This absence of a telos, however, liberates the wanderer's vision. We can even say that it is only now that he learns to *see*. He sees 'what is really going on in the world'. This *hypervision* is the result of his newly won freedom. The wanderer loses sight of the single horizon, but this loss opens up new visibilities for him.

His gaze itself wanders. Committed to change, and, yes, to what is novel, he does not linger in one place for too long. He distrusts the myth of 'depth' or 'origin'. He wanders across vast *surfaces*, turns towards the multicoloured appearances.

The wanderer's form of existence, however, does not resemble that of the hypercultural tourist. His way of walking still lacks the leisureliness that characterizes the tourist. And the world of the 'wanderer' is still peppered with deserts and abysses. The aphorism continues:

Such a man will, to be sure, experience bad nights, when he is tired and finds the gate of the town that should offer him rest closed against him; perhaps in addition the desert will, as in the Orient, reach right up to the gate, beasts of prey howl now farther off, now closer to, a strong wind arise, robbers depart with his beasts of burden. Then dreadful night may sink down upon the desert like a second desert, and his heart grow weary of wandering.[2]

Despite his faithfulness to the 'earth', Nietzsche remained a pilgrim. He did not yet know that hypercultural *being-here*. His path is a *via dolorosa*, which, as he had to do without 'God', only became more arduous, more painful.

Threshold

The keyhole in the threshold.

Peter Handke

For the most part, Heidegger's world remained dialectical. For him, hyperculture would be the end of culture as such.[1] He repeatedly laments the loss of the homeland [*Heimat*]. The media, too, are blamed for the disappearance of the homeland, and ultimately also for the disappearance of the world. They turn human beings into tourists:

> And those who *have* stayed on in their homeland? Often they are still more homeless than those who have been driven from their homeland. Hourly and daily they are chained to radio and television. Week after week the movies carry them off into uncommon, but often merely

common, realms of the imagination, and give the illusion of a world that is no world.[2]

The media only simulate a world, which is in truth 'no world' but only pretence. But what makes the world what it is? Where do we find the world if not in our ideas? Is there a realm of Being that is more primordial, even more world-like, than that 'common' realm of ideas? Heidegger has in mind a '*being-in-the*-world' that would reveal itself *antecedently* to the world of ideas and images. Heidegger uses the term 'facticity' to signify a being-*in* that comes *before* ideas. The images of the media apparently lack this primordial being-in-the-world. Heidegger sees the danger of the media in the fact that they de-facticize the world, that is, destroy the world's worldliness, the *being-in*-the-world that is antecedent to images and information.

In Heidegger's famous, tellingly titled lecture 'Why Do I Stay in the Provinces?' – which could very well be read as an anti-globalization pamphlet – there is an interesting hint about *Heidegger's world*. The world only *is* 'when one's own Dasein stands in *its work*'.[3] For someone watching a film or for a tourist, for those who do not *work* but only *behold*, the world does not exist. There world *is* where

> the gravity of the mountains and the hardness of their primeval rock, the slow and deliberate growth of the fir trees, the brilliant, simple splendour of the meadows in bloom, the rush of the mountain brook in the long autumn night, the stern simplicity of the flatlands covered with snow – all of this shifts and pushes.[4]

Heidegger's world is the *site* [*Ort*] that mediates a dialectical, rural and also *material* closeness. From this perspective, a hyperculture mainly made up of signs and images which shift and push each other in a de-sited side by side would be poor in world. Hyperculturality defacticizes, de-materializes, de-naturalizes and de-sites the world. The hypercultural simultaneity of diverse things also removes any 'stern simplicity' from the world. The *emptiness* of these 'flatlands covered with snow' gives way to the hyperspace of signs, forms and images.

We learn also about Heidegger's world from those 'things' which he repeatedly invokes as the bearers of world. In 'The Thing', Heidegger puts things into four categories: 1. 'the jug and the bench, the footbridge and the plow', 2. 'tree and pond . . . brook and hill', 3. 'heron and roe deer [*Reiher und Reh*], horse and bull', 4. 'mirror and clasp, book and picture, crown and cross'.[5] The nature of the thing, according to Heidegger, is that it reflects the world in itself. It is therefore worth taking a closer look at his collection of things. This will tell us which world Heidegger inhabited and wanted to inhabit. The arrangement of the things already suggests, as does – in the German – the alliteration, a strict and perspicuous order. The illusion of simplicity is also created at the level of syllables. Most of the named things have, typically enough, only one syllable. They thus appear *simple* even at the level of language. We get the impression that the strict simplicity of Heidegger's world is chiefly of a linguistic nature.

The first group of things, consisting of man-made objects, reflects the bright rural world. But it has little to do with the real world of the peasants. Rather, it is a *counter-world* designed by Heidegger as a reaction to a world dominated by modern technology, and then *projected* on to the world of the peasants. It *resembles very much* that romantic counter-world to which the tourists, criticized by Heidegger, are on their way. In a certain respect, *Heidegger* is himself a *tourist*, a pilgrim-tourist. After all, Heidegger, like the romantic tourist, is on a pilgrimage to an imaginary *There*.

The second and third groups of things represent a strict selection of organic and inorganic natural objects. Only native and harmless animals are included. There are also no insects, or vermin [*Ungeziefer*] (literally: animals not suitable to be sacrificed).[6] And the animals have to submit to alliteration and assonance, that is, to the linguistic order. Again, their names do not exceed two syllables, as if longer names would already destroy the strict, *simple* order of the world. The sole animal name with two syllables, heron [*Reiher*], is only included in the world of the monosyllabic animals on account of its assonance.[7] In his collection of things, Heidegger wouldn't want to include Benjamin's butterflies, with their multi-coloured, polysyllabic names: the 'Camberwell beauty', 'red admiral', 'peacock butterfly' or 'orange tip'.[8] It is also not a coincidence that Heidegger avoids composite words. They would be too complex for the simple order of the world. They would *hyphenate* the world, that is, destroy its 'stern simplicity'.

The fourth group is a set of cultural things. But unlike the things in the first group, which are also man-made, they not only have a use value but also a significant symbolic value. 'Crown' and 'cross' point towards a hierarchical and religious order. Significant, too, is the 'book'. Heidegger's world, in the end, is a world of the 'book', that is, a world with a closed, stable, repeatable order. Heidegger has little time for plurality or diversity. Heidegger's 'book' represents that 'nomos'[9] which brings 'each thing to that place where it belongs', keeps it 'in good order', 'straightened up and tidied'.[10] The image suggests that the order of the world is also visible and perspicuous. The image differs fundamentally from those media images which only simulate the world. Heidegger has in mind an image-like, mythical world in which, according to Flusser,

> Time puts everything in the place it deserves. If a thing leaves its place, then time puts it right: it rights it. The world is therefore full of meaning: full of Gods. This righting of the world by time is just ('dike') because it again and again puts everything in order ('cosmos').[11]

According to Flusser's classification, the hypertextual, hypercultural world would be a 'universe of points' in which there would no longer be any comprehensive order; it would therefore be a 'patchwork universe', one that maybe would consist of coloured panes or windows.

Why does Heidegger begin the last group of things with 'mirror and clasp [*Spiegel und Spange*]'? Their significance is probably clear only at a more abstract level. They introduce inwardness, an inwardness that opens up the inner space of the 'soul' or the 'house'. A mirror is not open. It is actually a counter-figure to the window, to the *window* of the hypertext. It reflects what is one's own. That is what constitutes its inwardness. The circularity, the closedness, of the clasp has the same effect. The clasp is the figure of the *return to oneself*. The alliteration, which is very pronounced in this fourth group, strengthens the impression of order and inwardness. The acoustic repetition creates an impression of almost regressive archaism.

Heidegger's world is also strangely mute or silent. There is no babel of voices. This silence intensifies the sense that the order of the world is simple. Like monads, the things reflect the world silently into the space ahead of them. They do not talk to each other. They do not look around. They have mirrors but no windows. '*Windowing*' or 'intertwingularity' would be wholly alien to Heidegger's things. All they signify is dispersal and decay.

Following Hölderlin, Heidegger points out the constitutive effect of the alien, that is, 'wandering' [*Wanderschaft*], for the formation of one's own.[12] But this 'wandering' is dramatically charged. The difference between what is one's own and the alien is also burdened by the emphasis Heidegger puts on it. The 'threshold' to the alien is as heavy and hard as stone, so to speak, making the crossing of the threshold a dramatic act. Of the threshold, Heidegger says:

> The threshold is the ground-beam that bears the doorway as a whole. It sustains the middle in which the two, the outside and the inside, penetrate each other. The threshold bears the between. What goes out and goes in, in the between, is joined in the between's dependability. The dependability of the middle must never yield either way. . . . The threshold, as the settlement of the between, is hard because pain has petrified it. . . . The pain presences unflagging in the threshold, as pain.[13]

Etymologically, the threshold [*Schwelle*] is the ground-beam of a house which, as a load-bearing element, also runs across the door. Thus, the threshold guards the inside of the house, and carries the house itself. In Heidegger, the threshold becomes an in-between space in which the inside and outside meet. Despite the between, Heidegger remained the philosopher of the house. His openness towards the outside is limited to the openness of the threshold, which *hesitates*. The threshold is, after all, turned towards the inside. The hypertextual or hypercultural absence of thresholds is wholly alien to Heidegger. He could have extended his collection of things by including the threshold: . . . *clasp, mirror and threshold*, they all guard the inwardness or the intimacy of the house.

The human of the future will most likely not be crossing thresholds, his face contorted in pain. The human of the future will be a tourist, smiling serenely. Should we not welcome that human as *homo liber*? Or should we rather, following Heidegger or Handke, remain a *homo dolores*, petrified into a threshold?[14] In his *Phantasien der Wiederholung*, Handke writes:

When you feel the pain of the thresholds, then you are not a tourist; the crossing is possible.[15]

NOTES

1 Carl Schmitt, *Land and Sea*, trans. Simona Draghici, Washington, DC: Plutarch Press, 1997, p. 59 (transl. amended).

Tourist in a Hawaiian Shirt

1 See *Der Spiegel*, 44/2000.

Culture as Home

1 Georg Wilhelm Friedrich Hegel, *Lectures on the Philosophy of History*, trans. J. Sibree, London: G. Bell and Sons, 1914, p. 237.
2 Ibid., p. 236.
3 Ibid., p. 235.
4 Ibid.
5 Georg Wilhelm Friedrich Hegel, *Lectures on the History of Philosophy*, Vol. I, trans. E. S. Haldane, London: Kegan Paul, Trench, Trübner & Co., 1892, p. 149 (transl.

amended).

6 Ibid.

7 Ibid., p. 150.

8 Johann Gottfried v. Herder, *Outlines of a Philosophy of the History of Man*, trans. T. Churchill, New York: Bergmann Publisher, 1800, pp. 489–90.

9 Johann Gottfried Herder, 'Another Philosophy of History for the Education of Mankind', in *Another Philosophy of History for the Education of Mankind and Selected Political Writings*, trans. Ioannis D. Evrigenis and Daniel Pellerin, Indianapolis/Cambridge: Hackett, 2004, pp. 3–97; here p. 30.

10 Ibid., p. 28.

11 Ibid., pp. 29–30.

Hypertext and Hyperculture

1 Theodor Holm Nelson, *Computer Lib/Dream Machines*, Redmond: Tempus Books of Microsoft Press, 1987, p. 30.

2 Ibid., p. 31.

3 Ibid.

4 Theodor Holm Nelson, *Literary Machines*, Edition 87.1, p. 1/16.

5 Ibid., p. 1/14.

6 Nelson, *Computer Lib/Dream Machines*, p. 31.

7 Ibid., p. 32.

8 Ibid., p. 142.

9 Ibid., p. 145.

10 Hyperculture, or hyperculturality, is a concept belonging to the *theory* and *philosophy of culture*. It differs from the concept of 'hyperculture' one finds in media theory and literary theory, which contrasts with book culture. See M. Klepper, R. Mayer and E.-P. Schneck (eds), *Hyperkultur: Zur Fiktion des Computerzeitalters*, Berlin: de

Gruyter, 1995, which contains exclusively contributions from the fields of media theory and literary theory that discuss hypertext, hyperfiction, science fiction, cyberpunk, cyberspace or virtual reality. Despite the title, then, it actually has very little to do with culture in the proper sense of the word, and indeed the volume does not contain any theoretical reflections on culture. 'Hyperculture' is merely used as an undefined collective term for computer-related phenomena.

11 Samuel Taylor Coleridge, 'Kubla Khan', in *Complete Poetical Works of Samuel Taylor Coleridge*, 2 vols, Oxford: Clarendon, 1912, Vol. 1, p. 295.

The Eros of Interconnectedness

1 Vilém Flusser, 'Die Zeit bedenken', in *Lab: Jahrbuch für Künste und Apparate* (2001/2), pp. 126–30.

2 Martin Heidegger, *Being and Time*, trans. John Macquarrie and Edward Robertson, Oxford: Basil Blackwell, 1962, pp. 437 and 435.

3 Ibid., p. 164.

Fusion Food

1 See George Ritzer, *The McDonaldization of Society*, London: Pine Forge Press, 2004. In Asia, McDonald's does not necessarily owe its success to rationalization. See J. L. Watson (ed.), *Golden Arches East: McDonald's in East Asia*, Stanford: Stanford University Press, 1997, and Joana Breidenbach, 'Globaler Alltag: Kann man Globalisierung verstehen?', in M. Kleiner and H. Strasser (eds), *Globalisierungswelten: Kultur und Gesellschaft in einer entfesselten Welt*, Cologne: Herbert von Halem Verlag, 2003, pp. 161–75.

2 Ulrich Beck, *What is Globalization?*, Cambridge: Polity Press, 2000, p. 47 (transl. amended).

3 Martin Heidegger, 'The Pathway', in Thomas Sheehan (ed.), *Martin Heidegger: The Man and the Thinker*, Chicago: Precedent Publishing, 1981, pp. 69–72; here p. 70.

Hybrid Culture

1 Hegel, *Philosophy of History*, p. 236.
2 Elisabeth Bronfen et al. (eds), *Hybride Kulturen: Beiträge zur anglo-amerikanischen Multikulturalismusdebatte*, Tübingen: Stauffenberg Verlag, 1997, p. 14.
3 Homi K. Bhabha, *The Location of Culture*, London: Routledge, 1994, p. 5.
4 Ibid.
5 Ibid., p. 7.
6 Martin Heidegger, 'Building Dwelling Thinking', in *Poetry, Language, Thought*, trans. Albert Hofstadter, New York: Harper & Row, 1971, pp. 141–59; here pp. 151f.
7 Ibid., p. 150.
8 Martin Heidegger, 'On the Essence of Ground', trans. William McNeill, in *Pathmarks*, Cambridge: Cambridge University Press, 1998, pp. 97–135; here p. 123.
9 Heidegger, 'Building Dwelling Thinking', p. 152. Cf. Bhabha, *Location of Culture*, p. 13.
10 John Cage uses the term *circus* (arena, square, large crossing) to name the friendly side by side, the simultaneity of heterogeneous sound events which lack inwardness, a centre or subjectivity. It is juxtaposed with the *focus* which gathers and *internalizes* [*ver-innerlicht*].
11 Dialectical is precisely that figure of thought that says identity is always already mediated by difference. In his well-known treatise *Identity and Difference*, to which Bhabha could very well have referred, Heidegger takes Hegel, among others, as one of the pioneers of this dialectic of identity and difference: 'For it is only the philosophy of speculative Idealism, prepared by Leibniz

and Kant, that through Fichte, Schelling, and Hegel established an abode for the essence, in itself synthetic, of identity. ... [S]ince the era of speculative Idealism, it is no longer possible for thinking to represent the unity of identity as mere sameness, and to disregard the mediation that prevails in unity. Wherever this is done, identity is represented only in an abstract manner.' Martin Heidegger, *Identity and Difference*, trans. Joan Stambaugh, New York: Harper & Row, 1969, p. 25. It is just this *abstract* thinking that the dialectic of identity and difference opposes.

12 Bhabha, *Location of Culture*, p. 162.

13 'Creolization' also denotes the process of cultural blending: 'Creolization also increasingly allows the periphery to talk back. As it creates a greater affinity between the cultures of center and periphery, and as the latter increasingly uses the same technology as the center, not least some of its new cultural commodities become increasingly attractive on a global market. Third World music of a creolized kind becomes world music; and world cities like New York, London, or Paris, in themselves partly extensions of Third World societies, come to exercise some of their influence as cultural switch-boards between peripheries (and semi-peripheries), not only as original sources.' Ulf Hannerz, *Cultural Complexity: Studies in the Social Organization of Meaning*, New York: Columbia University Press, 1992, p. 265.

14 Friedrich Schiller, *On the Aesthetic Education of Man*, trans. Keith Tribe, London: Penguin, 2016, p. 110 (transl. modified). It is not to be forgotten that creolization, too, remains tied to colonialism.

15 Ibid.

The Hyphenization of Culture

1 Bhabha, *Location of Culture*, p. 37.
2 Gilles Deleuze and Félix Guattari, *A Thousand Plateaus: Capitalism and Schizophrenia*, trans. Brian Massumi, Minneapolis: University of Minnesota Press, 1987, pp. 6f.
3 Ibid., p. 10.
4 Ibid.
5 See ibid., p. 15.
6 Ibid., p. 21.
7 *Meyers Konversationslexikon*, Leipzig and Vienna: Verlag des Bibliographischen Instituts, 1885–1892, Vol. 13, p. 790.
8 Deleuze and Guattari, *A Thousand Plateaus*, p. 25.
9 Ibid.
10 Ibid., p. 21.
11 Hyphen (Greek-Latin: 'together, in one') . . . 1. In ancient grammar, the combination of two words into a composite. 2. The dash used in a composite word.
12 Heidegger's hyphens are not *hyphen-like*, not additive. Rather, they are analytic or hermeneutic. Thus, they do not form compound words. Instead, a word is parsed into its semantic elements (e.g. 'dis-locate' or 'de-termine') in order to make its 'original' sense appear. A remark by Heidegger about his notion of 'being-in-the-world' is interesting in this context: 'The compound expression "Being-in-the-world" indicates in the very way we have coined it, that it stands for a *unitary* phenomenon' (*Being and Time*, p. 78).

The Age of Comparison

1 Friedrich Nietzsche, *Human, All Too Human*, trans. R. J. Hollingdale, Cambridge: Cambridge University Press, 1996, p. 24 (emph. B.-Ch. H.).
2 Friedrich Nietzsche, *Nachgelassene Fragmente 1875–1879*, Kritische Studienausgabe, Vol. 8, Munich: dtv, 1988,

p. 306. Foucault makes a similar remark on the 'philosophy of the future': 'Ainsi, si une philosophie de l'avenir existe, elle doit naître en dehors de l'Europe ou bien elle doit naître en conséquence de rencontres et de percussions entre l'Europe et la non-Europe' (*Dits et écrits*, ed. D. Defert and F. Ewald, Vol. III, Paris: Gallimard, 1994, pp. 622f.). ['Thus, if philosophy of the future exists it must be born outside of Europe, or equally born in consequence of meetings and impacts between Europe and non-Europe.' Michel Foucault, 'Michel Foucault and Zen: A Stay in a Zen Temple (1978)', in *Religion and Culture*, ed. Jeremy R. Carrette, trans. Christian Polac, New York: Routledge, 1999, pp. 110–14; here p. 113.]

3 Nietzsche, *Human, All Too Human*, p. 24.

The De-Auratization of Culture

1 Peter Handke, *Am Felsfenster morgens (und andere Ortszeiten 1982–1987)*, Frankfurt am Main: Suhrkamp, 1998, p. 280.

2 Walter Benjamin, 'The Work of Art in the Age of Its Technological Reproducibility', in *The Work of Art in the Age of Its Technological Reproducibility and Other Writings on Media*, trans. Edmund Jephcott and Harry Zohn, Cambridge, MA: Harvard University Press, 2008, pp. 19–55; here p. 21.

3 Martin Heidegger, 'Language in the Poem: A Discussion on Georg Trakl's Poetic Work', in *On the Way to Language*, trans. Peter D. Hertz, New York: Harper & Row, 1971, pp. 157–98; here p. 159. The English translation phrases the passage without using the expression quoted here. See Martin Heidegger, 'Die Sprache im Gedicht: Eine Erörterung von Georg Trakls Gedicht (1952)', in *Unterwegs zur Sprache*, Gesamtausgabe, Vol. 12, Frankfurt am Main: Klostermann, 1985, pp. 31–78; here p. 33.

4 Rilke, *the* poet of 'profundity', once asked himself 'whether perhaps all that we have in front of us and perceive and make a subject of exegesis and interpret is surface'. 'And what we call spirit and soul and love', he continues, 'is perhaps nothing but a quiet change on the small surface of a face close to us?' See Rainer Maria Rilke, 'Auguste Rodin', in *Sämtliche Werke*, Frankfurt am Main: Insel, 1965, pp. 135–280; here p. 212.

5 Benjamin, 'The Work of Art', p. 23.

6 Umberto Eco, 'Travels in Hyperreality', trans. William Weaver, in *Travels in Hyperreality: Essays*, San Diego: Harcourt Brace Jovanovich, 1986, pp. 22f.

Pilgrims and Tourists

1 Peter Handke, *Phantasien der Wiederholung*, Frankfurt am Main: Suhrkamp, 1983, p. 7.

2 Zygmunt Bauman, *Life in Fragments: Essays in Postmodern Morality*, Oxford: Blackwell, 1995, p. 82.

3 Ibid., p. 86.

4 Ibid., p. 87.

5 Ibid.

6 Thus Heidegger writes: 'They are going astray/But they do not get lost'. [Sie gehen in die Irre./Aber sie verirren sich nicht.] 'Holzwege ("Dem künftigen Menschen") (1949)', in *Aus der Erfahrung des Denkens*, Gesamtausgabe, Vol. 13, Frankfurt am Main: Klostermann, 1983, p. 91.

7 'Wege' [paths], ibid., p. 222 [Not/zögernden Dunkels/im wartenden Licht'].

8 'Ortschaft' [site-ness], ibid., p. 223 [mühsam langen Wege/in das immer Einfachere, Einfältige/seiner im Unzugangbaren/sich versagenden Ortschaft].

9 Bauman, *Life in Fragments*, p. 97.

10 Ibid.

1 Nelson, *Literary Machines*, p. 1/14.
2 Ibid.
3 Ibid., p. 1/15.
4 See ibid.: 'This is the mathematical usage, where connections are called "colored" if they are of different types.'
5 Ibid., p. 1/18.
6 Ibid., p. 0/3.
7 Ibid., p. 1/16.
8 Ibid., p. 2/34.

Odradek

1 The lens of hybridity offers a fresh perspective on Kafka. The protagonist Gregor Samsa also transforms into a shape that is a hybrid of human and animal. Kafka's narrative form is itself hybrid.
2 Franz Kafka, 'The Cares of a Family Man' [Die Sorge des Hausvaters], trans. Willa and Edwin Muir, in *Collected Stories*, London: Everyman's Library, 1993, pp. 183–5; here p. 183. On the interpretation of the proper name 'Odradek', see Byung-Chul Han, *Todesarten: Philosophische Untersuchungen zum Tod*, Munich: Wilhelm Fink, 1998, pp. 167–71.
3 Kafka, 'The Cares of a Family Man', pp. 183f.
4 Ibid., p. 184.
5 Ibid.
6 Ibid. (transl. amended).
7 Franz Kafka, 'An Old Manuscript', trans. Willa and Edwin Muir, in *Collected Stories*, pp. 171–3; here p. 171.
8 Ibid.
9 Ibid., p. 172.
10 Ibid.
11 Transl. note: 'coloured Self' in English in the original.

Hypercultural Identity

1 Transl. note: 'coloured Self' in English in the original.

Interculturality, Multiculturality and Transculturality

1 The Chinese (*wen-hua*), Japanese (*bun-ka*) and Korean (*mun-wha*) words for 'culture' are translations of the European concept. The European concept of culture was probably adopted and translated by the Japanese at the end of the nineteenth century, on the basis of Chinese sources. The first Chinese sign, '*wen*', means model, line, sign, writing or literature. The second sign, '*hua*', means transformation, change or metamorphosis. The modern term for 'chemistry' also contains the sign '*hua*'.

2 See Beck, *What is Globalization?*, p. 73.

3 Ibid.

4 Horst Reimann (ed.), *Transkulturelle Kommunikation und Weltgesellschaft: Zur Theorie und Pragmatik globaler Interaktion*, Opladen: Verlag für Sozialwissenschaften, 1992, p. 14. And ibid.: 'Intercultural communication between two or more cultural units that can be separated from each other with the help of certain criteria establishing their identities is by definition always a crossing of borders, but is mainly interested in mutual exchange (interculturation).'

5 Wolfgang Welsch, 'Transkulturalität – die veränderte Verfassung heutiger Kulturen', in Stiftung Weimarer Klassik a. o. (eds), *Sichtweisen: Die Vielheit in der Einheit*, Weimar: Edition Weimarer Klassik, 1994, pp. 83–122; here p. 84. Welsch draws on tropes such as 'hiking' and 'cross-border commuter' in order to characterize transculturality.

6 Ibid., p. 92.

On Lasting Peace

1 Immanuel Kant, 'Perpetual Peace', trans. H. B. Nisbet, in *Political Writings*, Cambridge: Cambridge University Press, 1991, pp. 93–131; here p. 98.

2 Ibid., pp. 99 and 105.

3 Ibid., p. 108.

4 Ibid., p. 113.

5 Ibid., pp. 113f.

6 Ibid., p. 112.

7 Ibid., p. 114.

8 The 'spirit of commerce' does not necessarily lead to de-nationalization. Indeed, it can be compatible with nationalism. Thus, Nietzsche says: 'What might be the motivation behind the demand for the separation of nations from each other, while everything else points towards their amalgamation? I believe dynastic interests and commercial interests go hand in hand in this.' Friedrich Nietzsche, *Nachgelassene Fragmente 1875–1879*, Kritische Studienausgabe, Vol. 8, Munich: dtv, 2009, p. 318.

9 Immanuel Kant, *Critique of Judgment*, trans. Werner S. Pluhar, Indianapolis: Hackett, 1987, p. 122.

10 Nietzsche, *Human, All Too Human*, p. 174.

11 Ibid.

12 Ibid., p. 175.

13 Friedrich Nietzsche, *The Gay Science*, trans. Josefine Nauckhoff and Adrian Del Caro, Cambridge: Cambridge University Press, 2001, p. 242.

14 Friedrich Nietzsche, *Nachgelassene Fragmente 1887–1889*, Kritische Studienausgabe, Vol. 13, Munich: dtv, 2009, p. 93.

15 Friedrich Nietzsche, *Nachgelassene Fragmente 1880–1882*, Kritische Studienausgabe, Vol. 9, Munich: dtv, 2009, p. 90. Nietzsche also believed that the 'interbreeding of many races' weakens the force of the will: 'Skepticism – is

the expression of a certain physiological condition as it necessarily arises in a major interbreeding of many races: the many inherited valuations are at war with each other, disrupt each other in their growth. The force that is lost most here is the will.' *Unpublished Fragments (Spring 1885– Spring 1886)*, trans. Adrian Del Caro, Stanford: Stanford University Press, 2020, p. 17. The will is tied neither to a particular valuation nor to the consistency or continuity of this valuation. Rather, the will allows for transformation. And the dense side by side of different perspectives need not provoke scepticism. It also creates space for a specific practice of freedom. Moreover, it prevents particular values from being seen as absolute or universal, something that produces a lot of conflict and violence. One of the fundamental traits of hyperculture is de-facticization, which enables one to project *oneself* beyond any inherited possibilities or valuations. Hyperculture thus promises more freedom and vitality. De-facticization also means de-naturalization. The different perspectives or valuations that present themselves in a hypercultural side by side are not tied to a 'race', 'soil' or 'site'.

Culture of Friendliness

1 Richard Rorty, *Contingency, Irony, and Solidarity*, Cambridge: Cambridge University Press, 1989, p. 73.
2 Ibid., p. 74.
3 Ibid., p. 80.
4 Ibid., p. 91.
5 Ibid., p. 92.
6 Ibid., p. 93.
7 Hans-Georg Gadamer, *Truth and Method*, trans. Joel Weinsheimer and Donald G. Marshall, London: Continuum, 2004, p. 14.
8 Ibid., p. 35.

Hyperlogue

1 Georg Wilhelm Friedrich Hegel, 'Konzept der Rede beim Antritt des philosophischen Lehramtes an der Universität Berlin (Einleitung zur Enzyklopädie-Vorlesung)', in *Enzyklopädie der philosophischen Wissenschaften III (Die Philosophie des Geistes)*, Werke, Vol. 10, Frankfurt am Main: Suhrkamp, 1986, pp. 399–417; here p. 416. [Transl. note: The German edition contains the draft of Hegel's inaugural lecture as an appendix; it is omitted in the English translation: *Philosophy of Mind*, trans. W. Wallace and A. V. Miller, Oxford: Clarendon, 2007.]

The Wanderer

1 Nietzsche, *Human, All Too Human*, p. 203.
2 Ibid.

Threshold

1 For Heidegger, 'culture' (lest we forget, a foreign word) *as such* has negative connotations. The expansion of the term 'culture', in the shape of a 'philosophy of culture' for instance, would be a first sign of decay. *Being and Time* (p. 222) already said that 'understanding the most alien cultures and "synthesizing" them with one's own' leads to 'an alienation [*Entfremdung*] in which its [i.e. Dasein's] ownmost potentiality-for-Being is hidden from it'. Hyperculture, which de-facticizes Dasein, leads to a radical alienation. Heidegger's ontology of Dasein could also be interpreted as an attempt to re-facticize philosophy itself, as a defence against that thinking which, 'without marrow, bones, or blood'[!], leads only a 'literary existence'. Martin Heidegger, *The Fundamental Concepts of Metaphysics: World, Finitude, Solitude*, trans. William McNeill and Nicholas Walker, Bloomington: Indiana University Press, 1995, pp. 11 and 75.

2 Martin Heidegger, 'Memorial Address', trans. John M. Anderson and E. Hans Freund, in *Discourse on Thinking: A Translation of* Gelassenheit, New York: Harper & Row, 1966, pp. 43–57; here p. 48.

3 Martin Heidegger, 'Why Do I Stay in the Provinces?', trans. Thomas Sheehan, in *Martin Heidegger: The Man and the Thinker*, Chicago: Precedent Publishing, 1981, pp. 27–30; here p. 27 (transl. modified).

4 Ibid. (transl. modified).

5 Martin Heidegger, 'The Thing', trans. Albert Hofstadter, in *Poetry, Language, Thought*, pp. 163–80; here p. 180.

6 Heidegger's world is also a Western world insofar as insects do not figure in it. No other culture is more hostile towards insects than Western culture. In Japanese haikus, for instance (and every haiku reflects the world in itself), insects abound. In contrast to Heidegger, Issa would want to include many insects in his collection of things. Here is one of his haikus: 'Into the wide world / the baby spiders scatter –/ Each makes a living.'

7 The literally monosyllabic things correspond to Heidegger's monosyllabic peasants: 'But in the evening during a work-break, when I sit with the peasants by the fire or at the table in the "Lord's Corner," we *mostly say nothing at all*. We smoke our pipes in silence. Now and again someone might say that the woodcutting in the forest is finishing up ... The inner relationship of my own work to the Black Forest and its people comes from a centuries-long and irreplaceable rootedness in the Alemannian-Swabian soil.' (Heidegger, 'Why Do I Stay in the Provinces?', p. 28; italics restored from German original). For Heidegger, hyperculture would be the definitive endpoint, even the total de-facticization, of life rooted in the soil. Hyperculture, incidentally, is very *rich in words*.

8 Walter Benjamin, *Berlin Childhood around 1900*, trans. Howard Eiland, Cambridge, MA: Harvard University Press, 2006, p. 52 (transl. amended).

9 Martin Heidegger, 'Letter on Humanism', trans. Frank A. Capuzzi, in *Pathmarks*, Cambridge: Cambridge University Press, 1998, pp. 239–76; here p. 274.

10 Martin Heidegger, *The Principle of Reason*, trans. Reginald Lilly, Bloomington: Indiana University Press, 1991, p. 61.

11 Vilém Flusser, 'Die Zeit bedenken', p. 127.

12 See Martin Heidegger, *Hölderlin's Hymn 'The Ister'*, trans. William McNeill and Julia Davis, Bloomington: Indiana University Press, 1996, p. 142: 'The appropriation of one's own is only as the encounter and guest-like dialogue with the foreign. Being a locality, being the essential locale of the homely, is a journeying [*Wanderschaft*] into that which is not directly bestowed upon one's own essence but must be learned in journeying.'

13 Martin Heidegger, 'Language', trans. Albert Hofstadter, in *Poetry, Language, Thought*, pp. 185–208; here p. 201.

14 In the late Heidegger, as is well known, human beings are called 'mortals'. Death is thereby declared to be something positive, and thus transfigured. Part of de-facticization, by contrast, is the overcoming of the thrownness into death.

15 Handke, *Phantasien der Wiederholung*, p. 13.